Alpha to Omega

BEVÉ HORNSBY AND JULIE POOL

SHORT STORIES BY LAURA THOMPSON

STAGE 1

ACTIVITY PACK

HEINEMANN EDUCATIONAL

Foreword

Alpha to Omega was the first complete teaching programme based on structured, sequential, phonetic and linguistic concepts, to be published in this country.

Subsequent spelling lists and workbooks have emulated *Alpha to Omega* but never surpassed it. Being devised by a speech therapist with in-depth knowledge of phonetics and linguistics pertinent to the teaching of speech and language skills is what makes it so unique. In its final form, Frula Shear added her humour and knowledge of life and dyslexics to devising the games and sentences for dictation.

Although complete in itself, it is now felt necessary to reproduce many of the exercises in *Alpha to Omega* in workbook form, usable by the pupil, either in class or individual lessons and to expand these worksheets and games to provide additional material for the over-learning these people, both children and adults, need. Also included in the activity pack are exercises on other aspects of learning which Dr. Hornsby, in her twenty years of teaching experience, has found to be lacking in persons with specific learning difficulties/dyslexia.

Thus, there will be material suitable for reading or dictation at the initial stages of consonant/vowel/consonant words, of consonant digraph and blend words and incorporating essential sight words 'was', 'said', 'you'. Beyond this level there is plenty of commercially produced reading material available.

Games and exercises for improving auditory perception, visual perception, directional confusion, eye/hand coordination and general knowledge will form an integral part of the activity pack.

We hope it will prove as useful and helpful as *Alpha to Omega* has been and it is intended to be used in conjunction with *Alpha to Omega* as it can never replace it.

Heinemann Educational Publishers
Halley Court, Jordan Hill, Oxford OX2 8EJ
A Division of Reed Educational & Professional Publishing Ltd
MELBOURNE   AUCKLAND   FLORENCE
PRAGUE   MADRID   ATHENS   SINGAPORE   TOKYO
SAO PAULO   CHICAGO   PORTSMOUTH (NH)
MEXICO   IBADAN   GABORONE   JOHANNESBURG
KAMPALA   NAIROBI

ISBN 0 435 10383 0

Copyright © Heinemann Educational Books 1989
First published 1989
97 98 99 14 13 12

The worksheets may be reproduced by individual teachers without permission from the publisher. All other material remains © Heinemann Educational Books and may not be reproduced in any form for any purpose without the prior permission of Heinemann Educational Books.

Design: The FD Group Ltd, Fleet, Hants
Illustrations: Alison Baxter
Printed in Great Britain by
Athenaeum Press, Gateshead, Tyne and Wear

Acknowledgements

The author and publisher would like to thank the following for permission to reproduce copyright material:
HMSO Publications for the road signs on Sheet 79, © Crown copyright

Laura Thompson for the short stories:
Nug and Nog, Tom and Ned and the pets,
Tom and Ned and the fox, Ned's pet,
Tom and the dog, What a mess!
The lost fish (1&2), Tom – a star is born,
Tim in the fog.
and for the poem 'Summer Holiday'.

Gill Kenny for the story: Putting the sounds together

Contents

Alpha to Omega (4th Edition) Page Reference		Sheet Number
	Teacher's notes	
	Useful Games, Equipment and Workbooks	
19	Learning the alphabet	1
19	Rainbow alphabet	2
19	Tracking the alphabet	3
20–2	Learning the sounds	4
	Learning the shapes	5a–c
22–3	The story of c	6a–b
22–3	Tracking for vowels	7
24	Putting sounds together	8a–b
24	Tracking for words	9
27	Madcap lot – A Rhyming Poem	10
27	Verbs	11
27	Proofreading	12
27	Short vowels worksheet	13
245–8	Days of the week – Poem	14
245–8	Day train	15a–b
	Days of the week – Tracking	16
	Nug and Nog – A story	17
30	Letter search	18
30–2	'sh' or 'ch' – initial sound	19
30–2	'sh' or 'ch' – final sound	20
30–2	'sh' or 'ch' – medial sound	21
	Student form to mark sound heard	22
30–2	'sh' or 'ch' worksheet	23
30–2	'wh' or 'th' fill 'em ups	24
30–2	'wh', 'th', 'sh' or 'ch' fill 'em ups	25
	Tom and Ned and the pets – A story	26
	Tom and Ned and the fox – A story	27
	Ned's pet – A story	28
	Tom and the dog – A story	29
	What a mess! – A story	30a–b
28–34	Blends fill 'em ups	31
28–34	Blends sorting worksheet	32
28–34	Blends fill 'em ups	33
28–34	*The lost fish* (1) – A story	34
28–34	"Shooting Stars" – A consonant blends board game	35a–b
47	*The lost fish* (2) – A story	36
	Sequencing	37a–b
51	Sight words for reading and spelling	38a–b
35–7	Assimilation fill 'em ups	39
35–7	'when' or 'went' fill 'em ups	40
	Hampton Court maze	41
35–7	"Up, up and away" – An assimilation board game	42a–b
38	Word sums mix 'n' match	43
40	City of London maze	44

Alpha to Omega (4th Edition) Page Reference		Sheet Number
43–51	'r' is such a helpful letter	45a–b
43–51	Word apartments: an 'ar', 'er', 'or' worksheet (sound separate)	46
43–51	'ar', 'er', 'or' fill 'em ups	47
43–51	Word sums	48
50	Word sums mix 'n' match	49
46	Writing for meaning	50
54	'want' or 'what' fill 'em ups	51
52–3	Wanda the wicked witch	52
52–3	Wanda's tracking	53
55	'w' fill 'em ups	54
19–57	*Tom – A Star is Born* – A story	55a–e
249–50	Months of the year worksheet	56
	Months and seasons worksheet	57
	Months of the year – tracking	58
245–8	*Summer Holiday* – A days of the week story	59a–b
58	'll' bricks	60
64	'ss' bricks	61
69	'ff' bricks	62
58–70	Flossy Words	63
58	*Tim in the fog* – An 'll' story	64
60	'they' or 'there' fill 'em ups	65
60	Short forms roundabouts	66
60	Short forms roundabouts	67
60–1	Short forms roundabouts	68
60–1	Short forms roundabouts	69
64–6	'ss' fill 'em ups	70
70	'of', 'off' or 'for' fill 'em ups	71
73	'c', 'k', or 'ck' fill 'em ups	72
73	'ck' or 'nk' fill 'em ups	73
73–4	'ed', 'ing', or 'et' fill 'em ups	74
75	'f' and 'th', 'v' and TH'	75
75	'th' not 'f' or 'v'	76
75	Words you need to know	77
75	Words you need to know	78
75	The Highway Code	79
75	Talk skills	80
76–9	'e' can be magic too	81
76–9	Magic 'e' fill 'em ups	82
80	Statements into questions	83
80–1	Questions into statements	84
88–9	Statements into questions	85a–b
90–1	Statements into questions – practising 'wh' words	86
92–106	Soft 'c' and 'g'	87
98	'k', 'c' or 'ck' fill 'em ups	88
107–8	'to be' + 'ing' – making the present continuous	89
	Checklist for *Alpha to Omega*, Stage One	90a–c

Skills Encouraged

Skills	Sheet numbers
Appreciation of letters with two sounds	6
Association	57
Association of Grapheme to Phoneme	4
Auditory Discrimination	4, 13, 19, 20, 21, 23, 24, 25, 31, 32, 33, 39, 40, 46, 47, 60, 61, 62, 71, 73, 75, 76, 81, 82
Cloze Procedure	11, 13, 23, 24, 25, 31, 33, 39, 40, 43, 46, 47, 50, 51, 54, 60, 61, 62, 63, 65, 70, 71, 72, 73, 74, 76, 82, 88
Comprehension	10, 17, 26, 27, 28, 29, 30, 34, 36, 55, 59, 64
Copying	5, 11, 15, 32, 33, 45, 50, 54, 56, 60, 61, 62, 65, 70, 72, 73, 88
Correction of Faulty Sound Production	19, 20, 21, 23, 24, 25, 75, 76
Deduction	48, 49, 56
Dictation	8, 10, 17, 45
Direction	59
Eye-Hand Coordination	3, 5, 7, 9, 41, 43, 44, 58
Figure-Ground Discrimination	3, 7, 9, 16, 18, 53, 58
Formal vs. Informal Register	66, 67, 68, 69
Game	35, 42
General Knowledge	41, 44, 79
Gestalt Function (parts into whole)	43, 48, 49
Grammar	11, 51, 65, 66, 67, 68, 69, 71, 74, 83, 84, 85, 86, 89
Independent Reading	8, 10, 17, 26, 27, 28, 29, 30, 34, 36, 45, 55, 59, 64, 77, 78, 87
Left to Right Orientation	3, 7, 9, 16, 53, 58
Letter Orientation	1, 2, 3
Manual Dexterity	1, 2, 5
Memory	87
Multi-kinaesthetic Discrimination	1, 2
Paired Reading	6, 8, 14, 23, 45, 52, 55, 56, 77, 78
Proofreading	12, 76
Reading and Writing for Meaning	11, 12, 26, 27, 28, 29, 30, 34, 36, 43, 50, 54, 60, 61, 62, 65
Rhyming	10, 14, 46, 59, 63
Sequencing	1, 2, 3, 9, 15, 16, 37, 43, 48, 49, 53, 56, 58
Spelling	38, 77, 78
Suffixing	74
Talk Skills	37, 64, 80
Time Exercise	3, 7
Transformation	83, 84, 85
Visual Discrimination	3, 4, 7, 9, 13, 16, 18, 23, 24, 25, 31, 32, 33, 39, 53, 58, 60, 61, 62, 79, 81
Visual Perception	41, 44
Vocabulary Building	19, 20, 21, 38, 77, 78

Teacher's notes

This book has been created as a companion volume to *Alpha to Omega*. Some of the worksheets are taken directly from *Alpha to Omega* and are presented here in a larger format with more space for the students' own responses.

The following are instructions for specific worksheets or games and are numbered to show to which sheet they refer.

1 **Learning the alphabet** It is essential to have a set of capital letters, preferably wooden ones, for students to spread out on the table and put into alphabetical order. If the whole alphabet is too difficult, start with half the alphabet.

   Play games with the students, such as finding the right letter when it is called out.

   Students can colour in this page.

2 **Rainbow alphabet** This worksheet is a direct continuation of 'Learning the alphabet'. Capital letters, preferably wooden, should be placed on the table in alphabetical order in a rainbow. Ask the students to find the middle of the alphabet (between M and N). Now ask the students to colour in the worksheet making the vowels red and the other letters blue. Ask them to put a red stripe on 'Y' to show it is a part-time vowel.

3 **Tracking the alphabet** Ask the students to cross off each letter in alphabetical order as they come to it. They must always track from left to right and must not be allowed to backtrack. When possible, they might enjoy timing themselves with a stopwatch for this exercise.

4 **Learning the sounds** The students should join each letter to the picture representing the letter's sound. They should say aloud both the sound of the letter and the object in the picture.

5 **Learning the shapes** The students should draw over and copy the patterns to help with their handwriting. Two special sheets follow on which they can practise writing letters. The first includes an alphabet to copy and help with 'd' and 'b'.

6 **The story of c** This story should be 'pair read' with or read to the students to help them understand the two sounds which 'c' makes.

7 **Tracking for vowels** Ask the students to cross off each vowel (and semi-vowel) as they come to it. They must always track from left to right and must not backtrack. When possible, they might enjoy timing themselves with a stopwatch for this exercise.

8 **Putting sounds together** These brief stories should be read as paired reading by teacher and students simultaneously. Afterwards, test them for comprehension by asking questions about what has happened. This should be done verbally.

   These stories can be used later for further dictation.

9 **Tracking for words** Give the students a red pen or pencil and ask them to draw a circle around each word they find. There are 24 consonant-vowel-consonant words hidden in this tracking and at least seven other sight words which they should have learned by now (see *Alpha to Omega*, p.24). They should track from left to right and not backtrack.

   Ask them to count the number of words they have found.

   See if they can find the alphabet.

10 **Madcap lot** *A rhyming poem for reading and dictation*. Ask the students to read this poem and tell you which words rhyme. A series of comprehension questions follow the poem. These questions should be answered both verbally and in writing. When you have collected in this sheet, use it for dictation.

11 **Verbs** Read the directions for this exercise to the students. Ask them to read each sentence, to select the appropriate verb from those at the top of the page and to write it in the space provided. The sentences should be copied by the students into their exercise books.

   A shorter version of this exercise is on page 27 of *Alpha to Omega*.

12 **Proofreading** *Consonant-vowel-consonant words*. Read the directions to the students. Ask them to write the missing word or words just above each sentence in the place where it/they belong(s). Then they should write the corrected sentence on the line(s) below.

   A shorter version of this exercise is on page 27 of *Alpha to Omega*.

13 **Short vowels worksheet** Ask the students to read the sentences and to fill in the missing vowels. They are all short vowel sounds.

14 **Days of the week** *A poem for paired readings*. Read this with your students as paired readings. Then ask them to complete the exercises which follow, especially the Day Train.

15 **Day Train** Ask the students to cut out the cars of the train and place them in order on the track. They might enjoy colouring the train. When they have finished, they should write the days of the week on the lines provided at the bottom of the sheet.

16 **Days of the week – tracking** The days of the week (Monday to Saturday) are hidden in order three times in this tracking. Ask the students to circle each day of the week going from left to right on each line. There is one day of the week hidden on each line. They should not backtrack or miss any out. Also hidden are the abbreviations for the days of the week. Ask them to find these if they have learned them. They are not in order.

17 **Nug and Nog** *A story*. Ask the students to read this story. When they have finished, ask them to divide a page in half and to put everything they know about Nug on one half and everything they know about Nog on the other half. They can either draw or write it. Then ask them to read the questions about 'Nug and Nog' and to answer them both verbally and in writing in complete sentences.

18 **Letter search** Ask your students to circle the letters and to write the ones they have found in their exercise books. Then they should write them in alphabetical order and write the missing ones underneath. (There are 15 letters hidden in this picture. They are b, c, d, e, g, h, i, j, n, o, p, t, u, w, y.) Now ask them to see how many words they can make using only the letters in the picture. (To date 77 words have been found.)

19 **'sh' or 'ch'** Initial sound. This sheet is the first in a series of three; they are strictly for auditory discrimination. The students should *not* be asked to read or spell these words. They should only be asked to listen to the words and whether they have heard 'sh' or 'ch'. The teacher should read the lists, one at a time to the student. At the end of this series of sheets on sheet 22 there is a check form which can be used by the students to tick which sound they hear.

20 **'sh' or 'ch'** *Final sound*. See 19 above.

21 **'sh' or 'ch'** *Medial sound*. See 19 above.

22 **Student form – to mark sound heard** This form can be used by the students to tick off which 'sh' or 'ch' sound they have heard.

23 **'sh' or 'ch' – worksheet** As some of the words in this exercise are quite difficult, it would be advisable for the teacher to read these sentences aloud with the students, allowing them to fill in the blank spaces with 'sh' or 'ch'.

24 **'wh' or 'th' fill'em ups** The students should read each sentence and fill in 'wh' or 'th' as appropriate.

25 **'sh', 'ch', 'wh' or 'th' fill'em ups** This worksheet is a final test or revision of the consonant digraphs 'sh', 'ch', 'wh', and 'th'. It should be done by the students when these digraphs are thoroughly established.

26 **Tom and Ned and the pets** This story takes the students to reading and using consonant digraphs. It includes the sight word 'was'. It should be read aloud by the students. Questions to test comprehension follow. These should be answered both verbally and in writing.

27 **Tom and Ned and the fox** This story includes the sight words 'said' and 'was'. See 26 above.

28 **Ned's pet** See 26 above.

29 **Tom and the dog** This story includes the sight words 'said', 'was', 'will' and 'began'. See 26 above.

30 **What a mess!** In this story the students practise recognizing blends, 'ed' endings and 'what'. See 26 above.

31 **Blends fill'em ups** Ask the students to read these sentences and to choose one of the words above each sentence to complete it. They should underline the word and write it in the space in the sentence. Then write the completed sentence in their exercise book.
   This exercise is on page 34 of *Alpha to Omega*.

32 **Blends** *A sorting worksheet*. Ask the students to read the list of words and to write each word on a line beneath its blend.

33 **Blends fill'em ups** See 31 above.

34 **The lost fish (1)** *A story using blends and assimilation*. Comprehension questions at the end of this story should be answered both verbally and in writing after the story has been read aloud by the students.

35 **Shooting Stars** *A consonant blends board game*. This game should be played after your students have learned the consonant blends in *Alpha to Omega* (pages 28–34). it is a game for two more players.
   Equipment: One or two dice and a counter for each player. If you are using two dice, the smaller number must be subtracted from the larger number.
   Instructions: Each player throws one dice. The player with the highest number goes first. If a player lands on a star, he/she must say the sound of the letters and say a word beginning with that sound. Then he/she must put the word in a sentence. If he/she cannot do this, he/she will be destroyed by the shooting star and must start again. The first player to reach home is the winner.

36 **The lost fish (2)** See 34 above.

37 **Sequencing** Ask your students to cut out these pictures and put each set in their correct order. The sheets can be coloured in and put on card for durability.

38 **Sight words** *For reading and spelling*. Cut out each word and put it on a card. The students should learn one word each week – or day, if they can manage it. They should practise reading it each day and should learn the first six words thoroughly for reading and spelling before going on to the others. Use the read, spell, cover, spell again with eyes closed, write, check' technique to help imprint the word on the students' minds.

39 **Assimilation fill 'em ups** Ask the students to read these sentences and to choose one of the words above each sentence to complete it. They should underline the word and write it in the blank space.

   This exercise is on page 39 of *Alpha to Omega*.

40 **'when' or 'went' fill 'em ups** Ask the students to read each sentence and to choose 'when' or 'went' to complete it. They should write the one chosen in the blank space and copy the completed sentences in their exercise books.

41 **Hampton Court Maze** An eye–hand coordination exercise. Ask your students to help this family out of the maze.

42 **Up, Up and away** *An assimilation game*. This is a game for two or more players to be played after learning about assimilation in *Alpha to Omega* (pages 35–37).

   Equipment: A counter for each player and his/her exercise book.

   Instructions: Each player takes a turn to climb the ladders, starting at the bottom of 'nd' and going from bottom to top of each ladder until he/she reaches to top of 'ng'.

   To go up the ladders, each player must think of a word for each step and write the word in his/her exercise book. If the player cannot find a word, he/she misses a turn.

43 **Word sums mix 'n' match** Ask your students to complete the words by drawing a line between the two parts. The first one has been done. Then they should write out the completed words in the spaces below. After this they should read the sentences and fill in the missing parts of the words. They should write the completed sentences in their exercise books.

44 **City of London maze** See 41 above.

45 **'r' is such a helpful letter** These pages are a good introduction to 'ar', 'er' and 'or'. They should be read as paired reading, or students can read them aloud on their own. Later the sentences can be used for dictation. Students might enjoy colouring in the large letters.

46 **Word apartments** *An 'ar', 'er', 'or' worksheet (sound separate)*. Ask your students to read the words in each window. All the words in each window belong in one sentence. The first word in each sentence has been filled in. Students should read the sentences and write in the missing words. They should write the completed sentences in their exercise books.

47 **'ar', 'er', 'or' fill 'em ups** In this worksheet the students need fill in only 'ar', 'er' or 'or' to complete the words. They should read the sentences and fill in the missing sounds.

48 **Word sums** Ask the students to choose an ending from the three provided for each word. They should then write the new word on the line opposite.

49 **Word sums mix 'n' match** Ask your students to match the beginnings to the endings and write the new words after the equals (=) sign. The words are 'darling', 'sparkler', 'platform', 'garden', 'army', 'target', 'carpet', 'hardly', 'market', 'alarm', 'report'.

50 **Writing for meaning** Ask your students to complete the words in the first part of the worksheet. The answers are 'target', 'carpet', 'market', 'alarm', 'garden', 'hardly', 'party'. In the second part of the worksheet the students are asked to unscramble the sentences and write them out correctly.

   This exercise is on page 46 of *Alpha to Omega*.

51 **'want' or 'what' fill 'em ups** Ask your students to read the sentences and to write 'want' or 'what' in the blank spaces so that the complete sentences make sense. The students should then copy the completed sentences onto the lines provided.

   A shorter version of this exercise is on page 54 of *Alpha to Omega*.

52 **Wanda the wicked witch** Read this passage together with your students (paired reading) after they have learned the 'w' rules on pages 52–56 in *Alpha to Omega*.

53 **Wanda's tracking** Ask your students to find the 'w' words hidden in the tracking. They should always track them left to right and should not backtrack. They should circle all the 'w' words and read them aloud when they have finished. The answers to this tracking are provided over the page. Ask them to track from the top left corner to the bottom right corner. They should find WANDA THE WICKED WITCH.

   A suggestion for using this tracking is to provide your students with three different coloured pencils or markers and ask them to circle each of the different types of 'w' words learned with a chosen colour.

   This sheet should be used only after all the 'w' rules on pages 52–56 in *Alpha to Omega* have been taught.

v

Wanda's tracking

```
W A N T B P S Q R W A S P T L G K M E
S A V M W H A T J P S N W A S H Z C I
R I N W A R F B I K W A R M D U T O L
W A R D V S E H W O R D T U D M O W U
G R E W A R D L P I Y E Q W O R K V J
B T W O R T H V L R W A R N U M O T Y
S I M A R W H A T E V E R K N P O V B
W O R L D U H E M L S R T O W A R D S
Y N O T H N K O W A T C H A H P L S N
I R W A S E N A Z I U S I L W A N D R
W H A T M O N W A T C H P G U G V C O
R I V Q W O R K B K I K L W O R M R H
W O R L D J V Y P L S B E T O W A R D
R O F W A S P T Q U W A R D H A X T E
W A N T B I Z M W O R D I V W R L P V
F O M D W H A T E V E R U S L I M D E
P A W A S H R I L T Y W A R M X T D B
B I L A W O R L D J E R L W A S O C R
W A N T G T O K D W O R T H Y F I W H
```

54 **'w' fill 'em ups** Ask your students to read the sentences and fill in the blank spaces with 'a', 'ar' or 'or' to complete the words. They should then write the complete form on the lines provided.

55 **Tom – a star is born** *A story in chapters.* This story covers the teaching in *Alpha to Omega* to page 57. It should first be 'pair read' with the students, then they should try to read it on their own and the teacher should ask them questions about their reading. Questions for comprehension have been included which should be answered both verbally and in writing. Questions for discussion are only suggestions and should be ad lib.

56 **Months of the year** This worksheet is to help the students in associating the months of the year. It should be 'pair read', then students should select the month(s) of the year necessary to complete the blanks and copy the month from the list at the top of the page.

57 **Months and seasons** Provide your students with four coloured pens – brown for autumn, black for winter, green for spring, and blue for summer. They should use the appropriately coloured pen to underline the months that go together and draw a line from each month to the picture of the season it belongs to.

58 **Months of the year – tracking** Ask the students to put a circle around each month of the year and each abbreviation. The months are hidden twice within the tracking. The months are in sequence but the abbreviations are jumbled. As always, tracking must be done from left to right.

59 **Summer holiday** *A days of the week story.* The words used in this story, except for the days of the week, are in *Alpha to Omega* as far as the end of the 'w' rules (page 56). It includes one sight word, 'our'. The days of the week are given for recitation on page 245 of *Alpha to Omega*. The students can be encouraged to make their own diary of a week, not necessarily in rhyme. Comprehension questions are included as both a verbal and written exercise.

Discussion can arise, e.g. as to what the rash might be, or what direction is North Sands, etc. Some lead questions have been included on the sheet.

60 **'ll' bricks** Ask your students to read the words in the bricks; then they should read the sentences below and fill in the blank spaces with a word from one of the bricks. They should then copy the sentences into their exercise books.

61 **'ss' bricks** See 60 above.

62 **'ff' bricks** See 60 above.

63 **Flossy words** The students should match the words in each balloon with the sentence to which it belongs. The first word in each sentence has been done to avoid confusion.

64 **Tim in the fog** *An 'll' story.* This story should be read as paired reading. Comprehension questions following the story should be answered both verbally and in writing. Discussion should follow the story.

65 **'they' or 'there' fill 'em ups** The students should write in 'they' or 'there' in the appropriate blank spaces so that the sentences make sense. The sentences should then be copied into the students' exercise cooks.

A shorter version of this exercise is on page 60 of *Alpha to Omega*.

66 **Short forms roundabouts** The students here are asked to replace the verb with its short form. The first sentence has been done as an example. Each sentence should be rewritten on the lines provided below the original sentence.

The exercises for expanding short forms, scaling down to possessive pronouns and scaling down negatives follow the same procedure.

These exercises are in *Alpha to Omega* (pages 60–64).

67 **Short forms roundabouts** See 66 above.

68 **Short forms roundabouts** See 66 above.

69 **Short forms roundabouts** See 66 above.

70 **'ss' fill 'em ups** The students should read the 'ss' words at the beginning of the worksheet. Then they should read the sentences and fill in the blank spaces with the appropriate words. They should then copy these sentences into their exercise books.

A shorter version of this exercise is on page 66 of *Alpha to Omega*.

71 **'of', 'off' or 'for' fill 'em ups** The students should fill in the blank spaces with 'of', 'off' or 'for' to complete the sentences. These sentences should be copied into the students' exercise books.

A shorter version of this exercise is on page 70 of *Alpha to Omega*.

72 **'c', 'k' or 'ck' fill 'em ups** The students should write in 'c', 'k' or 'ck' to complete the sentences. These sentences should be copied into the students' exercise books.

A shorter version of this exercise is on page 73 of *Alpha to Omega*.

73 **'ck' or 'nk' fill 'em ups** The students should read the two lists of words aloud, e.g. 'back', 'bank'. Then they should read the sentences and fill in the blank spaces with 'ck' or 'nk'. The sentences should be copied into the students' exercise books.

74 **'ed', 'ing' or 'et' fill 'em ups** The students should complete each word with the necessary ending.

This exercise is on pages 73–74 of *Alpha to Omega*.

75 **'f' and 'th', 'v' and 'TH'** This is an explanatory sheet to help students who have difficulty differentiating these sounds in speech, and therefore in spelling.

76 **'th' not 'f' or 'v'** After the students have thoroughly learned the previous speech pattern, they should complete this worksheet. In the first part they should fill in the 'th' missing from each word and read the word *aloud*. Then they should proofread the paragraph in the second part and correct all the mis-spelled words.

77 **Words you need to know** This sheet should be 'pair read' by teacher and students, and then read independently by the students. They should learn to spell the word thoroughly using the 'read, spell, cover, spell again with eyes closed, write and check' technique to help imprint each word on the mind.

78 **Words you need to know** See 77 above.

79 **The Highway Code** This is primarily an information sheet for older students who are learning the Highway Code. Ask them to colour the signs in the appropriate colours. Help them to read the information and to learn the meanings of the signs.

80 **Talk skills** This picture is meant as a stimulus for discussion, and should lead to a written description of what is taking place. Students could write in the style of a newspaper reporter, a trial or police witness, or several students might act it out as a play.

81 **'e' can be magic too** This sheet acts as an intoduction to magic 'e', which is dealt with in much greater detail in *Alpha to Omega* (pages 76–88). The macron (¯) and the breve (˘), which indicate long and short vowels respectively, are introduced at this time as a clear marker for the students to help them distinguish between long and short vowels when they are written. Do not bother about 'e' itself as this way of making 'e' say its name is really only used in words of *more than one* syllable.

82 **Magic 'e' fill 'em ups** The students should choose one of the words above each sentence to fill in the blank and complete the sentence. The completed sentences should be copied into the students' exercise books.

A shorter version of this exercise is on page 79 of *Alpha to Omega*.

83 **Statements into questions** This worksheet asks the students to change the statements into questions using the auxiliary 'to do'; the first one has been done as an example.

This exercise is on page 80 of *Alpha to Omega*.

84 **Questions into statements** This worksheet asks for questions to be turned back into statements.

This exercise is on pages 80–81 of *Alpha to Omega*.

85 **Statements into questions** This worksheet asks the students to turn the statements into questions by adding a 'tag'. The first two have been done as examples.

This exercise is on pages 88–89 of *Alpha to Omega*.

86 **Statements into questions** Practising 'wh' words. This is another exercise for students to practise turning statements into questions by using 'question' words beginning with 'w'. The first has been done as an example.

A shorter version of this exercise is on pages 90–91 of *Alpha to Omega*.

87 **Soft 'c' and 'g'** This sheet is intended as an introduction to the softening effect of certain vowels on specific consonants. This concept is explained more fully in *Alpha to Omega* (pages 92–106). The students should read the nonsense verses and colour in the large letters at the top of the page.

88 **'k', 'c' or 'ck' fill 'em ups** Ask the students to complete these sentences by filling in the blank spaces with 'k', 'c' or 'ck'. They should copy these sentences into their exercise books.

A shorter version of this exercise is on page 98 of *Alpha to Omega*.

89 **'to be' + 'ing'** *Making the present continuous.* The students should change these sentences into the present continous tense by using the verb 'to be' and adding 'ing' to the verb. The new sentence should be written on the lines provided.

This exercise is on pages 107–108 of *Alpha to Omega*.

90 Checklist for *Alpha to Omega:* Stage One This checklist is to help the teacher keep a record of concepts learned as each student progresses through *Alpha to Omega*.

Useful Games and Equipment to Accompany *Alpha to Omega*

Pelmanism Pairs Games following the concepts in *Alpha to Omega* by Bevé Hornsby and Catriona Fitzgerald:

Syllables pairs game

Short Vowels pairs game

Consonant Blends – 3 pairs games
- 's' blends
- 'r' blends
- 'l' blends

Triple Blends pairs game

Assimilation pairs game

Regular Past Tense 'ed' pairs game

'ng' and 'nk' pairs game

'ar', 'or' and 'er' pairs game

Flossy Words – 3 pairs games
- 'l' or 'll'
- 'f' or 'ff'
- 'c' or 'ck'

Magic 'e' pairs game

Suffixing – 4 pairs games
- Double or not
- Magic 'e' – to drop or keep
- Double or drop 'e'
- Keep 'y' or change to 'i'

Countries and Capital Cities pairs game

These games are available in boxed sets or as a flat pack with perforations from The Hornsby Centre, 71 Wandsworth Common Westside, London SW18 2ED.

Spelling Games by Elizabeth Wood. Published by E. J. Arnold.

Wooden Alphabet Letters from Galt Toys, Cheadle, Cheshire.

A Stopwatch.

Pens in assorted colours.

Useful Workbooks for More Practice

Hear It, See It, Say It, Do It, Books 1, 2, 3 by Mary Atkinson, available from Cheerful Publications, 7 Oxley Close, Gidea Park, Romford, Essex RM2 6NX.

Exercise Your Spelling, Books 1, 2, 3 by Elizabeth Wood, published by E. J. Arnold.

Learning the alphabet

M Y N C
L P T
H I
A G V
R U F
O J D
X E B Q
S K W Z

Note to the teacher
Scatter wooden capital alphabet letters on the table. (Those made by Galt are ideal for this.) Play games to find the right letter when it is called out.

Rainbow alphabet

ABCDEFGHIJKLMNOPQRSTUVWXYZ

Note to the teacher
Ask your students to make a rainbow shape with the wooden alphabet letters, like the one on this page. Next ask them to colour the rainbow on this page, making the vowels red and the other letters blue, but putting a red stripe on 'Y' to show it is a part-time vowel.

Vowels are fully explained on page 22 in *Alpha to Omega* by Bevé Hornsby and Frula Shear.

Tracking the alphabet

Z	B	W	Y	A	D	B	O	P	H
C	F	G	D	J	M	V	E	X	U
S	R	F	L	N	G	I	Q	O	H
Y	X	Z	I	P	M	J	U	V	T
K	M	N	R	Q	L	U	T	W	N
T	V	M	X	Z	N	R	P	O	R
Q	T	P	Z	W	Q	S	V	R	U
Y	V	U	S	V	T	U	Z	Y	X
H	D	I	V	B	L	W	K	X	Y
Q	Y	R	F	Y	U	M	W	A	Z

Note to the teacher
Ask your students to cross off each letter in alphabetical order as they come to it. They should always track from left to right and are not allowed to backtrack. They could time themselves with a stopwatch.

Learning the sounds

Note to the teacher

It's time for your students to learn the sounds. Ask them to join each letter in the illustration to the picture which starts with the letter's sound. Please note that the picture for **x** is a fox (the sound appearing at the end rather than the beginning of the word).

Sounds are taught in *Alpha to Omega* pp. 20–2.

Learning the shapes

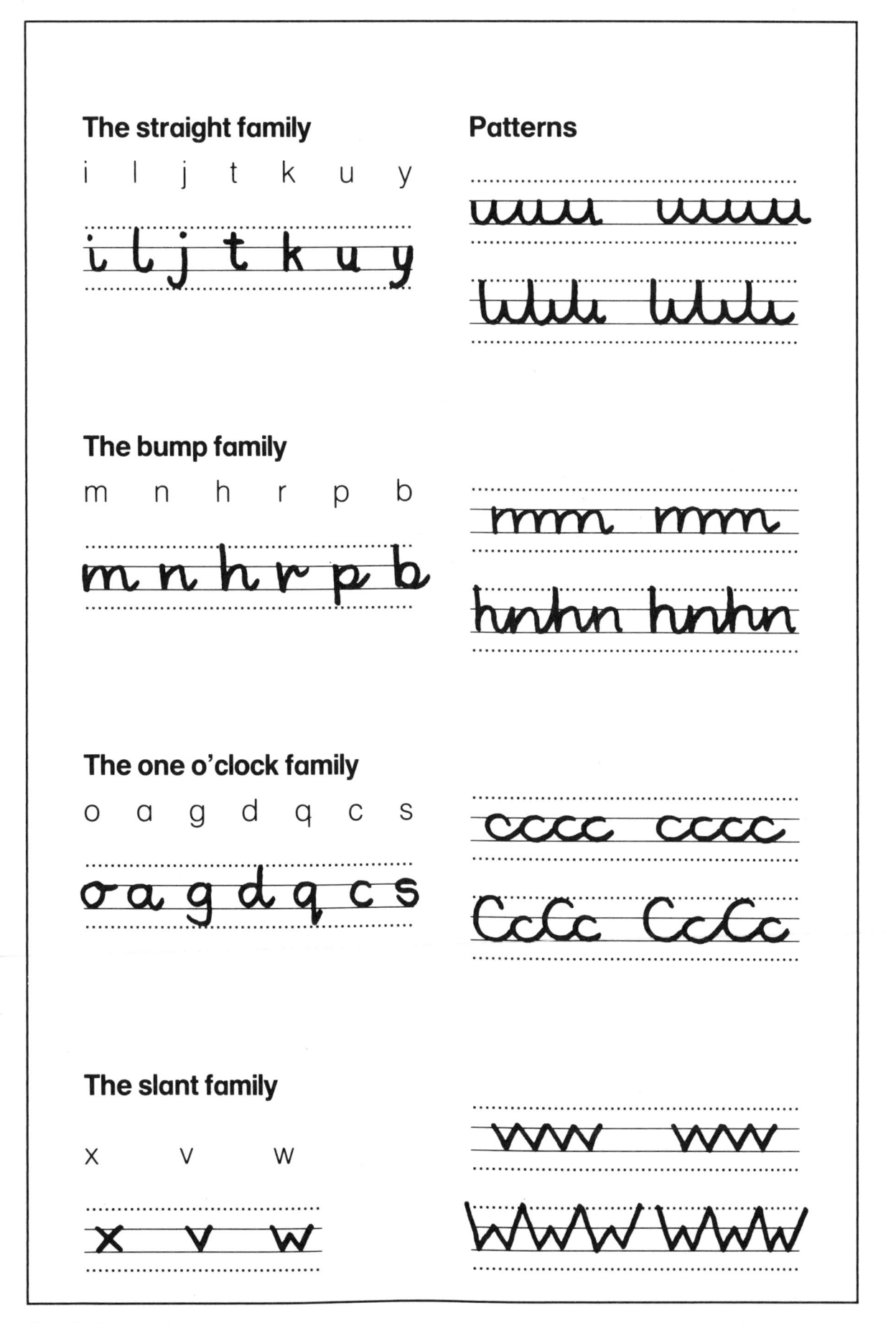

The straight family

i l j t k u y

i l j t k u y

Patterns

uuuu uuuu

tltltl tltltl

The bump family

m n h r p b

m n h r p b

mmm mmm

hnhn hnhn

The one o'clock family

o a g d q c s

o a g d q c s

cccc cccc

CcCc CcCc

The slant family

x v w

x v w

vvv vvv

wwww wwww

Note to the teacher
Help your students to improve their handwriting by asking them to practise the patterns above. If they are right-handed, ask them to slant their paper to the left; if they are left-handed, put the paper slightly to their left and slant it to the right so they are not crossing the mid-line. **Remind them that all letters start from the top.**

Do not ask your students to attempt more than six or seven writing patterns in a string. If you do, their hands will become tense and develop writer's cramp.

Alphabet to copy

abcdefghijklmnopqrstuvwxyz

Help with 'd'

cd cd cd cd cd cd cd

Help with 'b'

hb hb hb hb hb hb hb

Practice sheet

The story of c

Poor **c** was most unhappy.

When the alphabet was made, no one remembered to give **c** a sound. All the other letters had sounds.

But poor **c** did not know what to do so he sat silent in a corner.

Then along came his friends **k** and **s** and they were sorry for **c**.

"You can use our sounds," they said. **c** felt much happier.

Note to the teacher
Read the 'Story of c' to your students. Then 'pair read' it with each one.

When the vowels heard what **k** and **s** had done, they wanted to help too and began to quarrel.

Vowel **a**, who was a wise old vowel, had a good idea.

When **i** or **e** follow **c**, he can have **s**'s sound, and when **a**, **o** or **u** follow **c**, or another letter follows **c**, he can have **k**'s sound.

cat

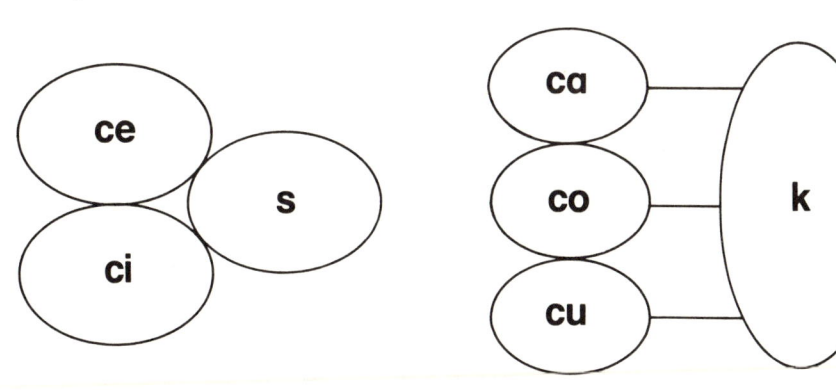

We will learn more about **c** saying **s** later. For now **c** will borrow **k**'s sound.

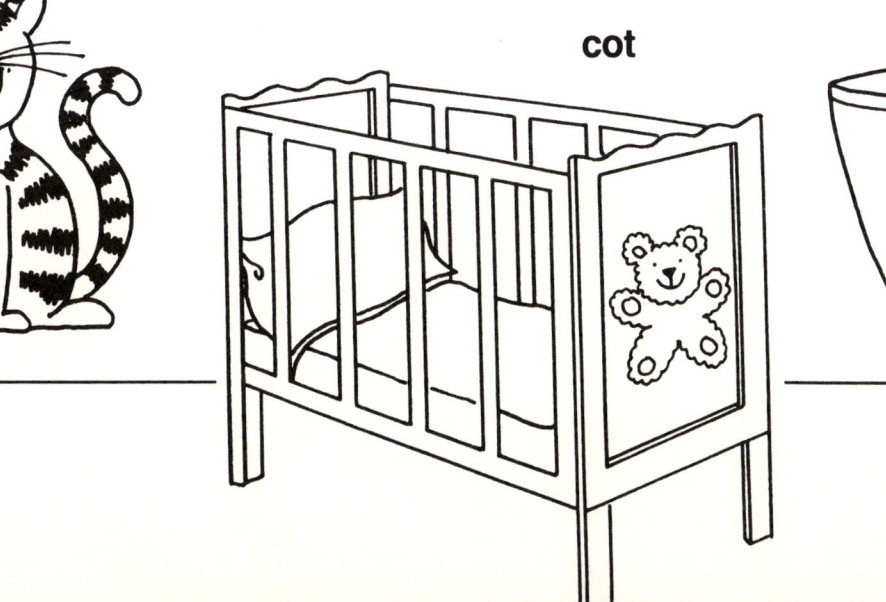

cot

cup

Tracking for vowels

(and semi-vowels)

a   e   i   o   u
y

b	z	l	a	k	m	p	r	e	s
t	i	f	g	y	n	o	v	j	q
u	w	d	a	x	y	z	e	f	h
r	i	j	l	o	m	n	q	u	y
a	b	e	c	i	d	o	k	p	u
r	a	x	e	w	i	z	o	v	u
n	m	d	a	e	i	o	u	f	j
a	g	e	q	i	z	o	t	u	s
k	o	l	u	w	i	x	e	y	a
a	l	o	b	u	d	e	v	i	z

Note to the teacher
Ask your students to cross off each vowel (and semi-vowel) as they come to it, always tracking from left to right.
Now play B and C short vowel pairs game.

Putting sounds together

The red fox sat on a pin.

Pop!

End of fox.

The fat pig sat on his hat.

End of hat.
Sad pig.

Note to the teacher
Explain that sounds can be put together to make words. 'Pair read' these brief stories with each student, then use them for dictation.

The man bit the dog.
I bet it bit him.

Sam got a cod
on his rod.

The cod is hot
in the pan.

Sam and Mum had
cod and jam.

Tracking for words

z	y	x	i	n	w	v	b	e	d	u	t
h	e	s	r	h	a	s	q	i	s	p	o
n	n	o	t	m	i	l	t	h	e	k	j
a	m	i	h	b	i	g	g	f	a	t	f
e	h	e	n	d	a	c	b	a	d	b	a
t	o	z	y	f	i	g	x	h	u	t	w
h	o	p	v	u	u	p	t	t	e	n	s
r	q	w	i	g	p	b	e	g	o	n	m
d	i	g	l	r	o	t	k	l	o	t	j
i	o	n	h	g	f	b	u	s	l	e	t
s	i	t	e	m	e	t	d	s	a	t	c
b	g	o	t	a	g	e	t	z	c	u	p

Note to the teacher
Ask your students to draw a circle round each word with a red pen or pencil. Count how many they find. Ask them to make up sentences using the words they have circled.

See if they can find the alphabet.

Madcap lot

Mum is Pam and Dad is Ted.
I am Sam and I am wed.
Nan is a big dog. It can beg.
It bit a madman on his leg.
Meg is a fox and it is fat.
It did a jig on Ron, the cat.
Sam had rum and Ted had ham.
Pam had a bun, but Meg had jam.
Ron bit Nan and Nan hit Jim.
Jim hit Tom and Dan hit him.
Kim is a hen, but not a pet.
Madcap Lot is a mad bad set.

Questions

1 Who is Pam? _____

2 Who is Dad? _____

3 What is Nan? _____

4 What can Nan do? _____

5 Who is fat? _____

6 Who had ham? _____

7 Who had a bun? _____

8 Who bit Nan? _____

9 Who hit Tom? _____

10 What is Kim? _____

Note to the teacher
Ask your students to read this poem out loud and to tell you which words rhyme. Ask them to answer the questions verbally, and then to write the answers down. Dictate the poem to your students.

Verbs

Verbs are **doing** words

| put | ran | has | sat | hid |
| see | went | hit | got | have |

1 Len _____ lunch at 2 o'clock.

2 Sam got home and _____ to bed.

3 Bob _____ wet in the rain.

4 We _____ to catch the bus.

5 Did you _____ the dog?

6 We _____ tea at 4 o'clock.

7 The cat _____ on the mat.

8 Pat _____ the ball with a bat.

9 Tom _____ the cash in a tin.

10 Mum _____ the fish in the pan.

Note to the teacher
Read the following to your students.
   Some of the verbs are missing from the sentences. All the missing verbs are listed above the sentences. Choose the correct verb and write it in the blank space in the sentence.

Proofreading

1 My pen is my bag.

2 I got the pen the shop.

3 Bob Ben can get it.

4 Can Sam go us?

5 Sam left it the desk.

6 Len has got dog, he has not got cat.

7 Is empty?

8 Ben can get pen that shop.

9 Is Len his desk?

Note to the teacher
Read the following to your students:
   What is wrong with these sentences? Read them and put them right by putting in the missing word or words. Then write out the sentences correctly on the line below the sentence.

Short vowels worksheet

a e i o u

1 P __ t s __ t on the f __ t c __ t.

2 The r __ t r __ n and bit the f __ t c __ t.

3 L __ t T __ d g __ t the n __ t.

4 Tom w __ t the n __ t and s __ t it in the b __ d.

5 The f __ sh s __ nks the sh __ p with a p __ n.

6 J __ m gr __ ns as he fl __ ps the t __ n.

7 The fr __ st can r __ t the l __ t.

8 It is a l __ ng dr __ p fr __ m the t __ p.

9 The r __ st is on the pl __ gs and the b __ mper.

10 Tom finds a g __ n, a d __ ck and a p __ mp in the j __ nk at the d __ mp.

Note to the teacher
Ask your students to fill in the missing vowels and then to read the sentences. Point out that all the vowels they have used make short vowel sounds.

Days of the week

Sunday

Monday

Tuesday

Solomon Grundy

Born on a Monday

Christened on Tuesday

Married on Wednesday

Took ill on Thursday

Worse on Friday

Died on Saturday

Buried on Sunday

This is the end

Of Solomon Grundy

Wednesday

Saturday

Friday

Thursday

Note to the teacher
Read this rhyme to your pupils and have them learn it. Then make cards of the days of the week for the children to arrange in order.

15a

Day train

Write the days of the week in order here:

_____

_____

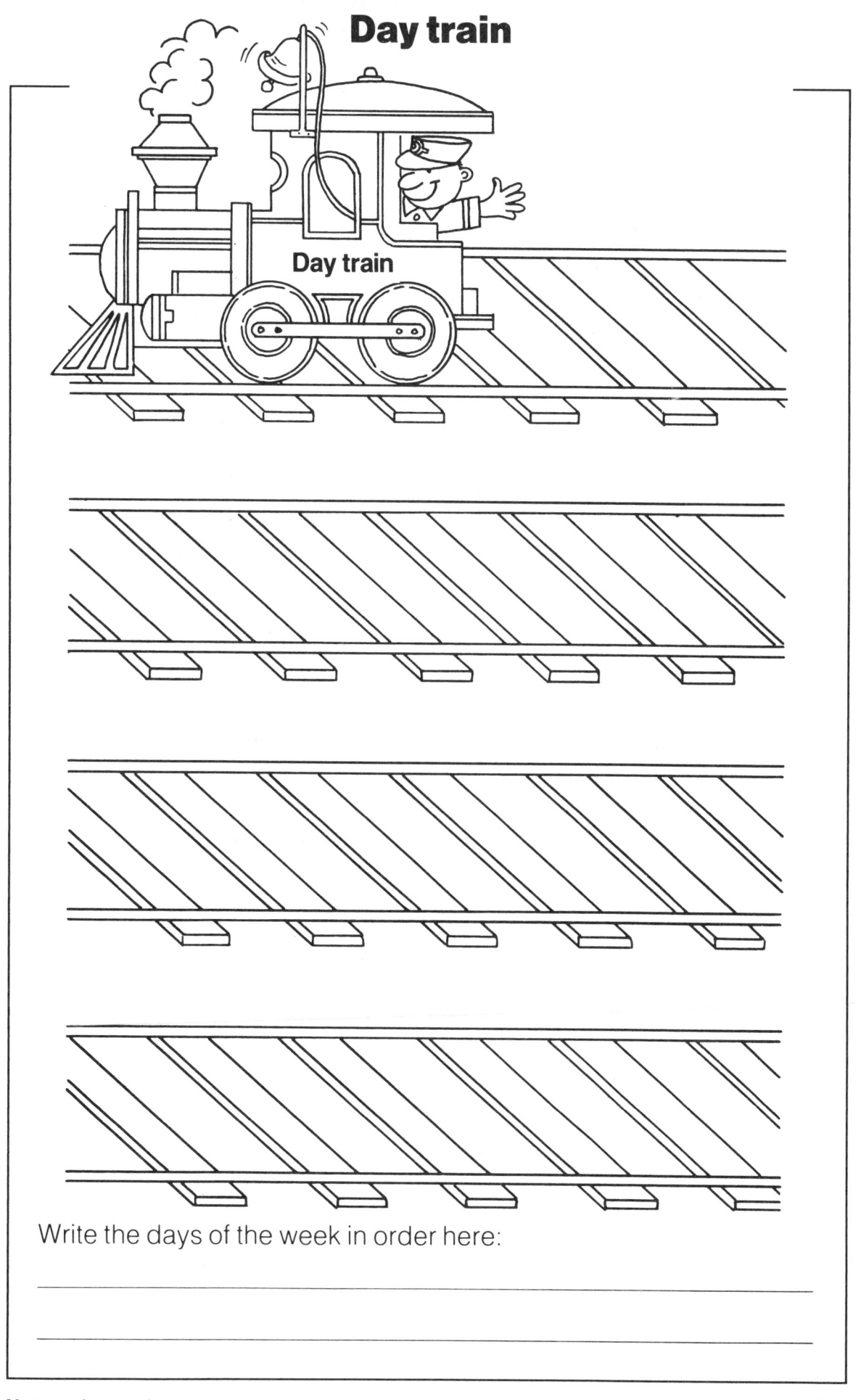

Note to the teacher
'Pair read' the poem on Sheet 14 with each student.

Day train
Ask your students to cut out the cars of the train on the next page and to place them in order on the track. When they have finished, ask them to write the days of the week on the lines provided at the bottom of the sheet.

15b

Days of the week — tracking

E	S	M	O	N	D	A	Y	S	A	T	N	D	A	Y
T	H	U	R	S	D	T	U	E	S	D	A	Y	M	O
W	E	D	N	E	S	D	A	Y	F	R	I	M	A	Y
S	U	N	T	O	W	Q	T	H	U	R	S	D	A	Y
B	M	O	N	F	R	I	D	A	Y	N	D	I	G	T
F	H	S	A	T	U	R	D	A	Y	E	W	E	D	P
R	O	T	U	E	S	P	L	S	U	N	D	A	Y	J
G	A	K	U	R	M	O	N	D	A	Y	S	W	E	D
T	U	E	S	D	A	Y	B	F	R	I	H	R	V	W
T	H	U	R	S	L	W	E	D	N	E	S	D	A	Y
X	E	T	H	U	R	S	D	A	Y	V	M	O	N	Z
F	R	I	D	A	Y	C	G	T	U	E	S	R	I	P
K	O	V	S	U	N	Q	S	A	T	U	R	D	A	Y
P	R	S	U	N	D	A	Y	V	S	A	T	B	M	T
T	E	S	U	M	O	N	D	A	Y	P	Z	F	R	D
S	U	N	O	T	U	E	S	D	A	Y	T	H	U	R
B	V	T	W	E	D	N	E	S	D	A	Y	S	A	T
C	X	D	T	H	U	R	S	D	A	Y	M	O	N	Z
Q	W	E	D	F	R	I	D	A	Y	T	U	S	P	H
V	L	K	S	A	T	U	R	D	A	Y	T	U	E	S
O	J	A	T	S	U	N	D	A	Y	T	H	U	R	S

Note to the teacher
Ask your students to circle each day of the week going from left to right on each line. Also hidden are the abbreviations for the days of the week.

Nug and Nog

Nug was a big man. Nog was not.
Nug had a cab, but Nog had a red van.
Nog did not hit the dog, but Nug did.
Nog fed his cat on cod.
Nug's cat was not fed.
Nug got up at ten but
Nog got up at six.
Nog did a job. He cut up logs.
Nug sat and had rum and buns and got fat.

Questions

1 Who was a big man?

2 Who had a cab?

3 Who hit the dog?

4 Who fed his cat?

5 Who got up at six?

6 Who sat and got fat?

7 What did Nug hit?

8 What did Nog's cat get?

9 What job did Nog do?

10 When did Nug get up?

Note to the teacher
Ask your students to read the story out loud. Ask them to answer the questions verbally, and then to write the answers down. Dictate the story to your students.

Letter search

How many letters can you find?

Note to the teacher
Ask your students to circle the letters on the picture and to write the ones they have found in their exercise books. Then they can write them in alphabetical order, and write the missing ones underneath.

Ask them to write down as many words as they can using only the letters in the picture.

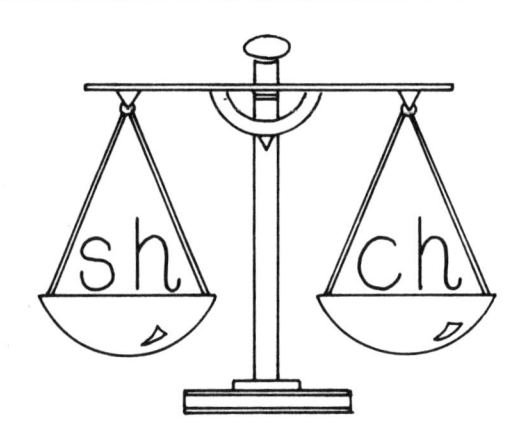

1 shuttle	**18** shimmering
2 chain	**19** change
3 chair	**20** short-sighted
4 shutters	**21** shaving
5 shameless	**22** chance
6 church	**23** shepherd
7 shot	**24** channel
8 shower	**25** chanting
9 challenge	**26** shiftless
10 shoulder	**27** chestnut
11 child	**28** shrivel
12 shovel	**29** chick
13 chamber	**30** chocolate
14 shouting	**31** shambling
15 champion	**32** chief
16 shifting	**33** shaky
17 cheese	**34** chunk

Note to the teacher
Ask your students to point to 'sh' or 'ch' when they hear these sounds at the beginning of the words on this sheet.
NB These words are for **auditory** discrimination only. Do **not** ask the students to read or spell them.
Discuss any words which students are not familiar with to improve vocabulary.

1	flash	**20**	furnish
2	match	**21**	lurch
3	punish	**22**	refresh
4	finish	**23**	arch
5	bench	**24**	relish
6	search	**25**	push
7	relinquish	**26**	inch
8	crunch	**27**	lunch
9	scorch	**28**	wash
10	extinguish	**29**	dish
11	entrench	**30**	birch
12	polish	**31**	crush
13	rich	**32**	fish
14	relish	**33**	church
15	March	**34**	wish
16	flinch	**35**	stitch
17	fresh	**36**	bush
18	punch	**37**	which
19	witch	**38**	flush

Note to the teacher
Ask your students to say whether they hear 'sh' or 'ch' at the end of the words on this sheet.
NB These words are for **auditory** discrimination only. Do **not** ask the students to read or spell them.
Don't forget to discuss any words which are unfamiliar to the students.

1	punishment	**19**	washing
2	enchantment	**20**	rushing
3	munching	**21**	achieve
4	fishing	**22**	reached
5	fashionable	**23**	pushing
6	luncheon	**24**	purchase
7	researcher	**25**	furnishing
8	polisher	**26**	refurbishing
9	relishing	**27**	matching
10	marching	**28**	refreshing
11	churchgoer	**29**	matchmaker
12	archbishop	**30**	Washington
13	marshmallow	**31**	richer
14	crunchy	**32**	wishful
15	itching	**33**	refreshment
16	dishes	**34**	flushed
17	touching	**35**	bunched
18	orchard	**36**	watchful

Note to the teacher
Ask your students which letters they hear in the middle of the words on this sheet.

NB These words are for **auditory** discrimination only. Do **not** ask the students to read or spell them.

Ask your students if they know what all the words mean. Discuss any they are unfamiliar with.

Student form – to mark sound heard

	Sheet 19: initial sound			Sheet 20: final sound			Sheet 21: medial sound	
	sh	ch		sh	ch		sh	ch
1	☐	☐	1	☐	☐	1	☐	☐
2	☐	☐	2	☐	☐	2	☐	☐
3	☐	☐	3	☐	☐	3	☐	☐
4	☐	☐	4	☐	☐	4	☐	☐
5	☐	☐	5	☐	☐	5	☐	☐
6	☐	☐	6	☐	☐	6	☐	☐
7	☐	☐	7	☐	☐	7	☐	☐
8	☐	☐	8	☐	☐	8	☐	☐
9	☐	☐	9	☐	☐	9	☐	☐
	sh	ch		sh	ch		sh	ch
10	☐	☐	10	☐	☐	10	☐	☐
11	☐	☐	11	☐	☐	11	☐	☐
12	☐	☐	12	☐	☐	12	☐	☐
13	☐	☐	13	☐	☐	13	☐	☐
14	☐	☐	14	☐	☐	14	☐	☐
15	☐	☐	15	☐	☐	15	☐	☐
16	☐	☐	16	☐	☐	16	☐	☐
17	☐	☐	17	☐	☐	17	☐	☐
18	☐	☐	18	☐	☐	18	☐	☐
19	☐	☐	19	☐	☐	19	☐	☐
	sh	ch		sh	ch		sh	ch
20	☐	☐	20	☐	☐	20	☐	☐
21	☐	☐	21	☐	☐	21	☐	☐
22	☐	☐	22	☐	☐	22	☐	☐
23	☐	☐	23	☐	☐	23	☐	☐
24	☐	☐	24	☐	☐	24	☐	☐
25	☐	☐	25	☐	☐	25	☐	☐
26	☐	☐	26	☐	☐	26	☐	☐
27	☐	☐	27	☐	☐	27	☐	☐
28	☐	☐	28	☐	☐	28	☐	☐
29	☐	☐	29	☐	☐	29	☐	☐
	sh	ch		sh	ch		sh	ch
30	☐	☐	30	☐	☐	30	☐	☐
31	☐	☐	31	☐	☐	31	☐	☐
32	☐	☐	32	☐	☐	32	☐	☐
33	☐	☐	33	☐	☐	33	☐	☐
34	☐	☐	34	☐	☐	34	☐	☐
			35	☐	☐	35	☐	☐
			36	☐	☐	36	☐	☐
			37	☐	☐			
			38	☐	☐			

Note to the teacher
Students can use this form to tick off the sounds they hear on sheets 19–21.

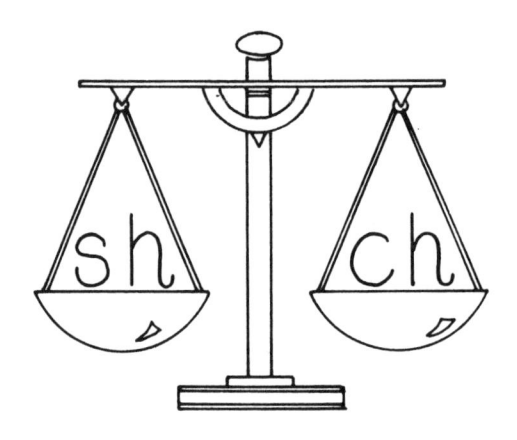

1 I wi____ I had a bun____ of flowers to give my mother. Flowers are a ____arming gift.

2 Let's go to wat____ the football mat____ when we finish our lun____. If we go now, we will avoid the ru____.

3 The furni____ings must mat____ when you refurbi____ the cottage.

4 The Ar____bishop visited your ____urch last Mar____ and met many fellow wor____ippers.

5 You cannot ru____ when you are fi____ing. The ____immering fi____ sear____ for fre____ food. Keep your rod from ____aking and they might bite. Then you have a cat____.

Note to the teacher
Read these sentences aloud to your students. Ask them to fill in the blank spaces with 'sh' or 'ch'.

'wh' or 'th' fill 'em ups
wh   th

1 _____ at is _____ at book?

2 _____ en did you find _____ at?

3 _____ at is not _____ at it looks like.

4 _____ ere did you go from _____ ere?

5 Did you see _____ o _____ at was?

6 _____ ich one of _____ ose do you want?

7 I want _____ is one.

8 _____ at is _____ at I want over _____ ere.

9 _____ en did you see _____ at film?

10 _____ y did you go _____ ere?

11 Pat was _____ ere. Did you see her?

12 _____ at did you see?

13 _____ ere did you see it?

14 _____ y are you late today?

Note to the teacher
Ask your students to write in the correct 'wh' or 'th' beginnings of the incomplete words.

'sh', 'ch', 'wh' or 'th' fill'em ups

wh   th   sh   ch

1 _____ at is my hat.

2 Come wi _____ me.

3 _____ ere did you go?

4 _____ ut the door.

5 I am sitting on a _____ air.

6 _____ ow me your book.

7 _____ at is your name?

8 _____ is is my home.

9 Let's have some fi _____ and chips.

10 You can have three wi _____ es at the wi _____ ing well.

11 She is very _____ in.

12 _____ is fi _____ is wet.

13 _____ at is in your hand?

14 _____ ow me whi _____ _____ op to go to for a hat.

15 _____ is is the _____ op wi _____ the wet fi _____ .

Note to the teacher
This worksheet is a final test or revision of the consonant digraphs 'sh', 'ch', 'wh' and 'th'. Only ask your students to complete the exercise when these digraphs are thoroughly established.

Ask them to choose the correct letters and to fill in the spaces so each sentence makes sense. Ask them to read the sentences out loud.

Tom and Ned and the pets

Tom and his pal Ned ran to get on the bus. It was a big red bus. Ned ran to the top of the bus and Tom sat by him.

Ned had a box in his bag. In Ned's box was a pet rat. Tom had no box but he had a tin. In his tin was a pet bug.

Ned let his rat run in his bag. Then he let it run in the bus. It ran to Tom's bag. Tom's bug hid in the tin in the bag, so the rat did not get it.

The rat then sat on Ned's lap but it began to nip Ned on the leg, so it had to go in the box.

Tom and Ned got off the bus and ran to the shop to get a bag of chips.

Questions

1 Who is Tom's pal? _____

2 Why did Tom and Ned run? _____

3 What was in Ned's box? _____

4 What did Tom have? _____

5 What was in it? _____

6 Where did Ned's rat run? _____

7 Whose leg did Ned's rat nip? _____

Note to the teacher
This story includes the sight word 'was'. Ask the students to read the story out loud. Ask them to answer the questions verbally, and then to write the answers down.

Tom and Ned and the fox

Tom had a pal, Ned. Ned had a pet fox. It was a red fox with a bad leg. He had to hop.

Ned hid his fox in the hut, but the fox was sad. Ned put a big box in the hut, but the fox was sad. Ned put a rug in the hut, but the fox was sad. Ned put a ham in the hut, but the fox was sad.

Dad saw the fox. "It is bad to put a fox in a hut," said Dad. "A fox has to be on the run. That is fun."

So Ned let the fox go, and he ran in the sun. He did not hop. Ned was sad, but the fox was not.

Questions

1 Who had a pet fox? _____

2 Why did the fox hop? _____

3 Who hid the fox in the hut? _____

4 What did he put in the hut for the fox? _____

5 Why was the fox sad? _____

6 Who let the fox go? _____

7 What did the fox do? _____

Note to the teacher
This story includes the sight words 'said' and 'was'. Ask your students to read the story out loud. Ask them to answer the questions verbally, and then to write the answers down.

Ned's pet

Ned was sad. He had no fox. He had no pet. His mum said, "Let us get a pup. A pup is a pet you can put in a hut. It will not be sad."

Mum and Ned got Rex. He had to be fed and led. He ran to the cat and the hens. He got on top of the bin. He hid in the bed. He got wet in the mud. He sat in his box and he sat on the rug and he sat on Mum's hat! What a lot he did! He was so fit.

He was Ned's pet and he was not bad. He was a pup.

Questions

1 Who was sad? _____

2 Why was he sad? _____

3 Who did he and Mum get? _____

4 Where did he run? _____

5 How did he get wet? _____

6 Where did he sit? _____

7 Who was Ned's pet? _____

Note to the teacher
This story includes the sight words 'said' and 'was'. Ask your students to read the story out loud. Ask them to answer the questions verbally, and then to write the answers down.

Tom and the dog

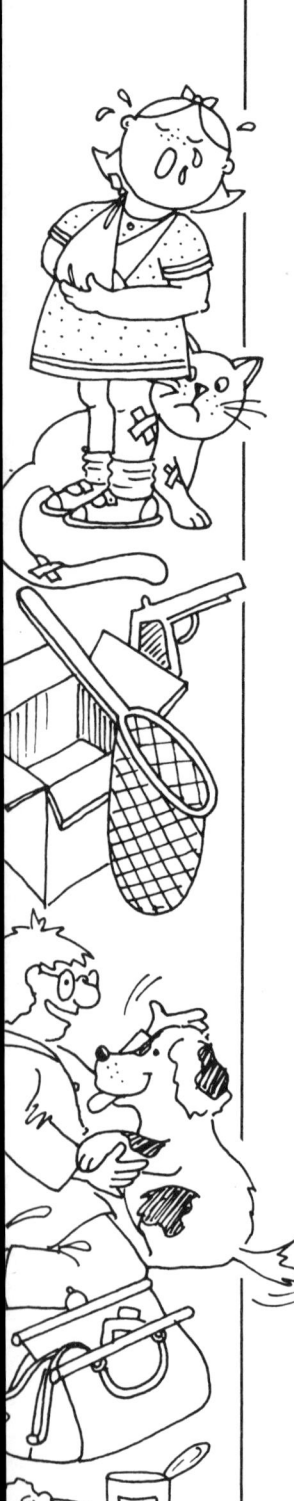

The dog bit Tom, it bit Jan and then it bit the cat.

Dad said, "We will get that dog as it is mad and bad." The men ran to get the dog. Ron had a gun, Pat had a net and Tim had a big box.

Then the vet got up to the dog. "He is a pup. He is not mad and he is not bad. He is hot and has had a fit," said the vet. "We will put him in my van and he can have a jab."

Tom was sad. The dog got his jab. He began to nod. He had a nap, then he sat up to beg, and was fed. He had a big hug. He was not bad and he was not mad.

Questions

1 Who bit Tom, Jan and the cat? _____

2 Who said that the dog was mad and bad? _____

3 What had Tim got? _____

4 What did the vet do with the pup? _____

5 Who had a big hug? _____

Note to the teacher
This story includes the sight words 'said', 'was', 'will' and 'began'. Ask your students to read the story out loud. Ask them to answer the questions verbally, and then to write the answers down.

What a mess!

Mum was in bed with a bad leg, so Dad put the twins, Dan and Tamsin, in the pram, strapped them in and went to the shops.

As he stepped on to the zebra crossing, a bus sped up to them and stopped in the mud just by the pram. Mud splashed over the pram and over Dad.

What a mess!

The twins began to cry and Dad felt ill, but he crossed over and went to Tesco. He had a big bag for the shopping under the pram as he had a lot on his list.

He kept the twins in the pram and they had a drink of milk in a cup. They spilt the milk in the pram and the blanket was wet.

What a mess!

Dad had a box on the pram for the shopping. He got a pot of jam, a bag of plums, three hot cross buns, a tin of red polish, three cans of Chum for the dog, Jelly Tots for the twins and six eggs.

Note to the teacher
In this story students will practise blends, 'ed' endings and 'what'. Ask them to read the story out loud, then to answer the questions verbally, and then to write the answers down.

Just as Dad got to the end of the egg shelf, Tamsin grabbed a box of eggs with her left hand and six eggs smashed up Dad's legs.

What a mess!

Dad went red but the twins began to clap. This was fun. They did not have such fun with Mum. Dad left the shop in a rush.

He pushed the pram, with the twins and the bag of shopping, up the hill. He began to pant. He was so hot that his jumper was wet.

What a mess!

Just as he got to the flat, a big dog ran out and jumped up, so that the bag fell off the pram. The jam ran from the jam pot on to the crushed plums and the buns. When Mum saw the shopping, she said,

(Can you guess?)

"What a mess!"

Questions

1 Why was Mum in bed?

_____

2 What did Dad have in the box for the twins?

_____

3 What did Tamsin grab with her left hand?

_____

4 What did Mum say when she saw the shopping?

_____

Blends fill'em ups

1 **grab**   **grog**   **glum**   **grin**
   Do not be so _____

2 **slop**   **slam**   **slim**   **slug**
   Jim dug up a _____

3 **plot**   **plop**   **prop**
   The film did not have much of a _____

4 **trim**   **trap**   **trip**   **tap**
   We went on the _____

5 **risk**   **rusk**   **desk**   **tusk**
   We must run the _____

6 **crest**   **crust**   **crisps**
   I wish I had a bag of _____

7 **just**   **rust**   **trust**
   If it is left in the wet, it will _____

8 **stop**   **stub**   **stun**
   When it is red, you must _____

9 **flags**   **flats**   **flaps**
   It is a big drop from the top of the _____

10 **exist**   **insist**   **exam**
   When do you get the results of the _____?

11 **slush**   **splash**   **thrush**
   When she went for a swim, fat Pam made a big _____

12 **felt**   **left**   **lift**
   We can go up in the _____

13 **held**   **help**   **helm**
   "I must get _____," he said.

Note to the teacher
Ask your students to read the sentences and then to choose one of the words above to finish each one. They should underline the word and write it in the blank space.

Blends — worksheet

stop   prop   spot   snap
crib   crab   spit   strum
spin   snag   three   step
pram   from   splint scrub
thrush splash snip   prod
frog   stub   fret   froth
split   scrap   stun   thresh
snug   span   crop   spud
scrum   thrash scram   cram
strap   strip   strut   splat

cr   **fr**   **pr**   **sn**

_____   _____   _____   _____
_____   _____   _____   _____
_____   _____   _____   _____
_____   _____   _____   _____

sp   **st**   **scr**

_____   _____   _____
_____   _____   _____
_____   _____   _____
_____   _____   _____

spl   **str**   **thr**

_____   _____   _____
_____   _____   _____
_____   _____   _____
_____   _____   _____

Note to the teacher
Ask your students to read the list of words and then to write each word on a line below its blend.

Blends fill'em ups

1 fret   frog   from   froth

The dog jumps _____ the bank into the pond.

2 snag   snap   snip   snug

The cat was as _____ as a bug in a rug.

3 span   spin   spot   spud

Tom has a _____ on his chin.

4 step   stop   stub   stun

Pat was at the bus _____ .

5 splash   splat   splint   split

The frog went _____ in the pond.

6 scrap   scram   scrum   scrub

Mum had to _____ the bin with Vim.

7 strap   strip   strum   strut

You cannot _____ on a drum.

8 thrash   three   thresh   thrush

The _____ sat on a twig.

Note to the teacher
Ask your students to read the sentences and then to choose one of the words above to finish each one. They should underline the word and write it in the blank space.

The lost fish (1)

Pam went to the shop to get cod for lunch. It was fresh cod.

Mum was not in, so Pam put the fish on a dish in the shed. She did not shut the shed.

Along crept the cat. He said, "I can smell fresh fish on that dish. Pam has left it in the shed, so I can help myself."

Just as the cat got the fish, Pam ran to shut the shed. The cat did not stop. He dashed to the pond.

Questions

1 Where did Pam go for the cod? _____

2 What was the cod for? _____

3 Where did Pam put the fish? _____

4 Who crept along and helped himself? _____

5 The cat got the fish. What did Pam do? _____

6 Where did he dash with the fish? _____

Note to the teacher
In this story students will practise blends and assimilation. Ask your students to read the story out loud, then to answer the questions verbally, and then to write the answers down.

Shooting stars

Note to the teacher
This is a consonant blends board game, to be played when your students have learned the consonant blends in *Alpha to Omega*, pp. 28–34. It is a game for two or more players. (See Teacher's Notes, p. iv, for directions on how to play.)

35b

The lost fish (2)

Pam ran to the pond. The cat did not let the fish go.

"Drop my fish," begged Pam, but the cat ran up a branch.

"Drop that cod," said Pam. The cat *did* drop it – into the pond with a splash. It sank in the mud.

That bad cat had lost the lunch. It was in the pond in the mud.

"We must have egg and chips," said Mum, "as we have no cod." She was mad. Pam was sad, and that cat was very bad!

Questions

1 Where did Pam run? _____

2 Did the cat let go of the fish? _____

3 Where did the cat drop the fish? _____

4 Where did the fish sink? _____

5 What did Mum and Pam have for lunch? _____

6 Who was mad? _____

Note to the teacher
Ask your students to read the story out loud. Ask them to answer the questions verbally, and then to write the answers down.

Sequencing

Note to the teacher
Ask your students to cut out these pictures and to put each set in the correct order.

37b

Sight words

was	are
have	said
they	you
about	before
came	come
could	down
here	like

Note to the teacher
These are sight words for reading and spelling. Students should learn one word each week, or each day if they can manage it.

little	look
made	make
more	new
now	only
our	over
other	out
right	some
their	there
two	want
who	were
what	when
where	which
your	old

Assimilation fill'em ups

1 jump   slump   stump

Tom can _____ up the step.

2 camp   cramp   clamp

I have _____ in my left leg.

3 think   drink   sink

Milk is a _____

4 munch   lunch   crunch

We crash into the stump with a _____

5 clench   bench   wrench

Let's sit on the _____ at the bus stop.

6 blend   bland   blond

My best pal is a _____

7 ramp   lamp   stamp

Run the van up the _____

8 bend   lend   mend

I cannot _____ you the cash.

Note to the teacher
Ask your students to read the sentences and then to choose one of the words above to finish each one. They should underline the word and write it in the blank space.

'when' or 'went' fill'em ups

1 We all _____ on a trip in the car.

2 I _____ to school on the bus.

3 _____ we _____ to see Grandma, I slipped and hit my head on the wall.

4 We _____ swimming in the pond.

5 _____ is my birthday?

6 Mummy and Daddy _____ on a trip to Finland.

7 Bring me a cup of tea _____ I wake up.

8 _____ can we have some sweets?

9 _____ must I go to bed?

10 We _____ to the shop _____ it was open.

11 I _____ to school on the bus by myself.

12 _____ Dad came home, we _____ to the park.

Note to the teacher
Ask your students to read the sentences and then to choose 'when' or 'went' to complete each one. They should write the chosen word in the blank space and then write the completed sentences in their exercise books.

Hampton Court maze

Can you get this family out of the maze at Hampton Court?

Do you know where Hampton Court is and who lived there long ago?

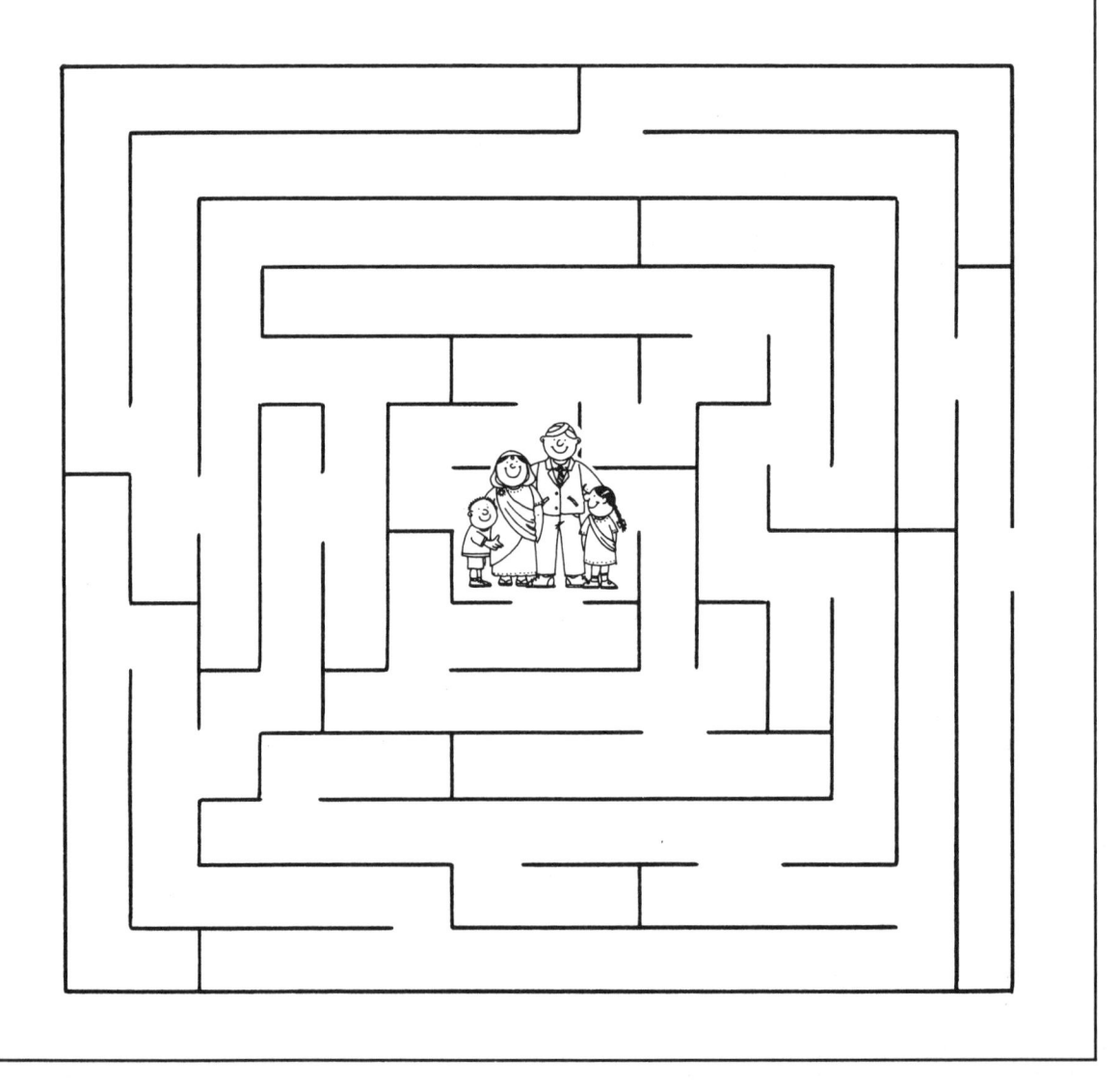

Note to the teacher
Ask your students to help the family out of the maze.–it will allow them to practise eye–hand coordination.

Up, up and away

nd **nt**

Start

Note to the teacher
This is an assimilation game for two or more players to be played when your students have learned about assimilation (see *Alpha to Omega*, pp. 35–7).

See Teacher's notes, p. v, for directions on how to play.

mp nk ng

Finish

Word sums mix 'n' match

up	ship
hun	nis
trum	to
flag	bush
rab	lem
grand	set
prob	bit
in	dred
ten	pet
am	ma

_____   _____

_____   _____

_____   _____

_____   _____

_____   _____

1 The cat _____ set the milk pan.

2 A hun _____ boys ran up the bank.

3 Can you play the _____ pet?

4 The rab _____ romped in the hay.

5 _____ ma is coming to tea today.

6 I had a prob _____ with my bag.

7 He went _____ to the bank for the cash.

8 The _____ ship is number one.

9 Ten _____ is her best game.

10 The boys sat in the hut during the _____ bush.

Note to the teacher
Ask your students to complete the words by drawing a line between the two parts, and then to write the completed words in the spaces provided.

Ask them to read the sentences, to fill in the missing parts of the words, and then to write the completed sentences in their exercise books.

City of London maze

Can you help this girl and boy to find their way out of the City of London? They went to find the Bank of England and have got lost in the maze of tiny streets with wonderful names like Ave Maria Lane, Bread Street, and Friday Street. Their mother is waiting for them, so please help.

Note to the teacher
More eye–hand coordination. Ask your students to help this boy and girl out of the maze.

'r' is such a helpful letter

ar or er

ar

Car words

The red car is sharp as a dart and has lots of charm but it is hard to get it to start with no spark.

'r' is such a helpful letter

Note to the teacher
'Pair read' the words with your students or ask them to read them out loud on their own. Ask them to colour in the large letters. Dictate the sentences.

More words and sentences are in *Alpha to Omega*, pp. 43 and 48. Ask the students to make their own crossword like the one in *Alpha to Omega*, p. 238

or

Sport words

Sport is fun but not in a storm with the wind in the north.

er

Mary, Mary, quite contrary
How does your garden grow
With rosemary, thyme parsley and mint
And camomile all in a row

Herb words

Her herbs were so perfect that her sister put them in a verse.

Word apartments

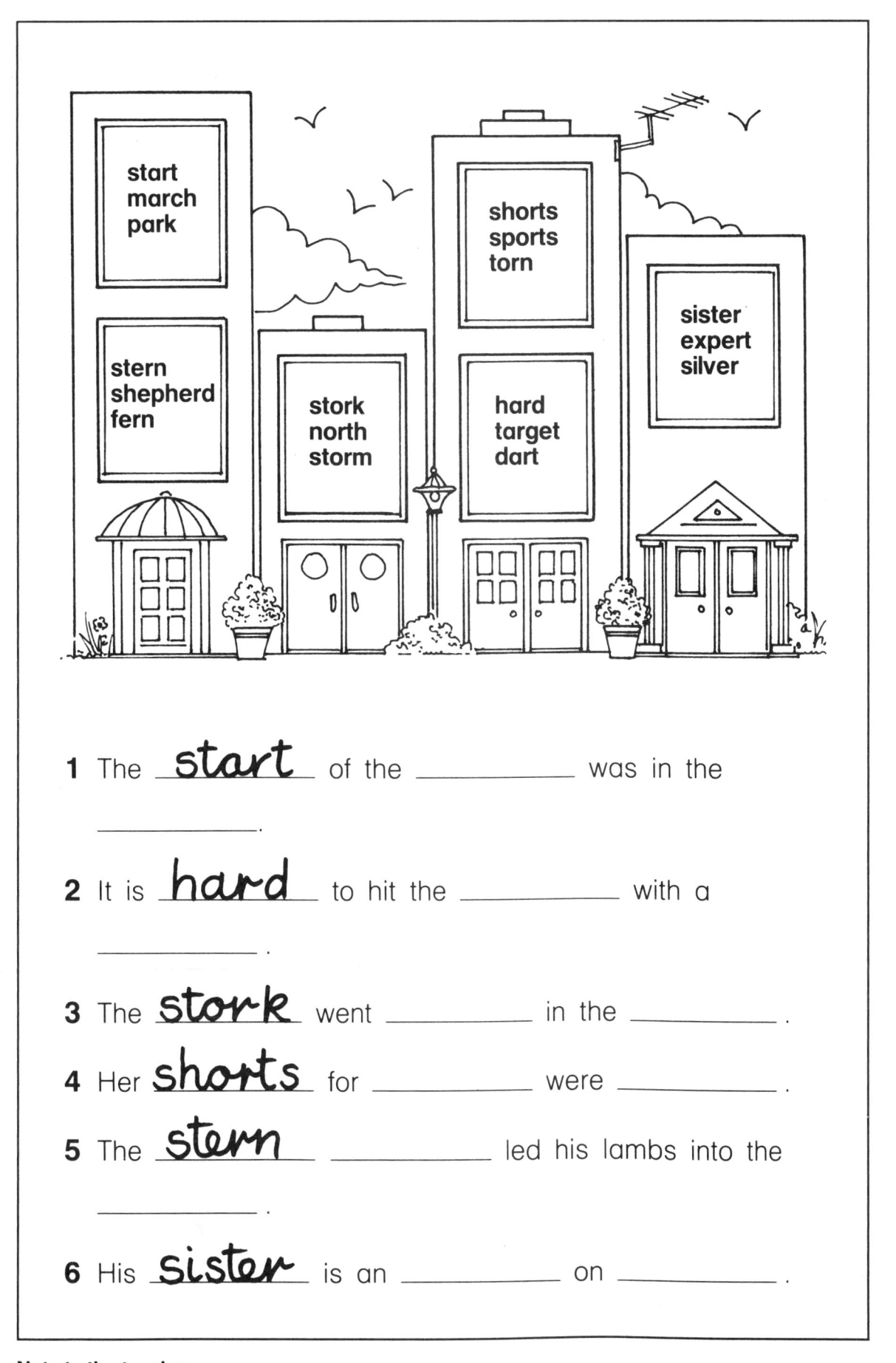

Building windows contain:
- start / march / park
- shorts / sports / torn
- stern / shepherd / fern
- stork / north / storm
- hard / target / dart
- sister / expert / silver

1 The **start** of the _____ was in the _____.

2 It is **hard** to hit the _____ with a _____.

3 The **stork** went _____ in the _____.

4 Her **shorts** for _____ were _____.

5 The **stern** _____ led his lambs into the _____.

6 His **sister** is an _____ on _____.

Note to the teacher
This is an 'ar', 'er', 'or' worksheet. Ask your students to read the words in the windows and then to use them in the sentences below. (All the words in each window belong in one sentence. The first word in each window has been written into each sentence.) They should then write the completed sentences in their exercise books.

46

'ar', 'er', 'or' fill'em ups

'ar' says **ar** as in **art**
'er' says **er** as in **mother**
'or' says **or** as in **born**

1 The bus st _____ ts from the riv _____ bank.

2 Your c _____ is on the f _____ bank of the riv _____ .

3 The ship in the p _____ t has a sh _____ t b _____ th.

4 My sist _____ is sm _____ t. She is top of h _____ f _____ m.

5 H _____ broth _____ was b _____ n on a f _____ m.

6 Your moth _____ is bett _____ at making butt _____ .

7 I can see the N _____ th St _____ .

8 H _____ fath _____ did not both _____ to ring.

Note to the teacher
Ask your students to read the sentences and then to fill in the missing sounds.

Word sums

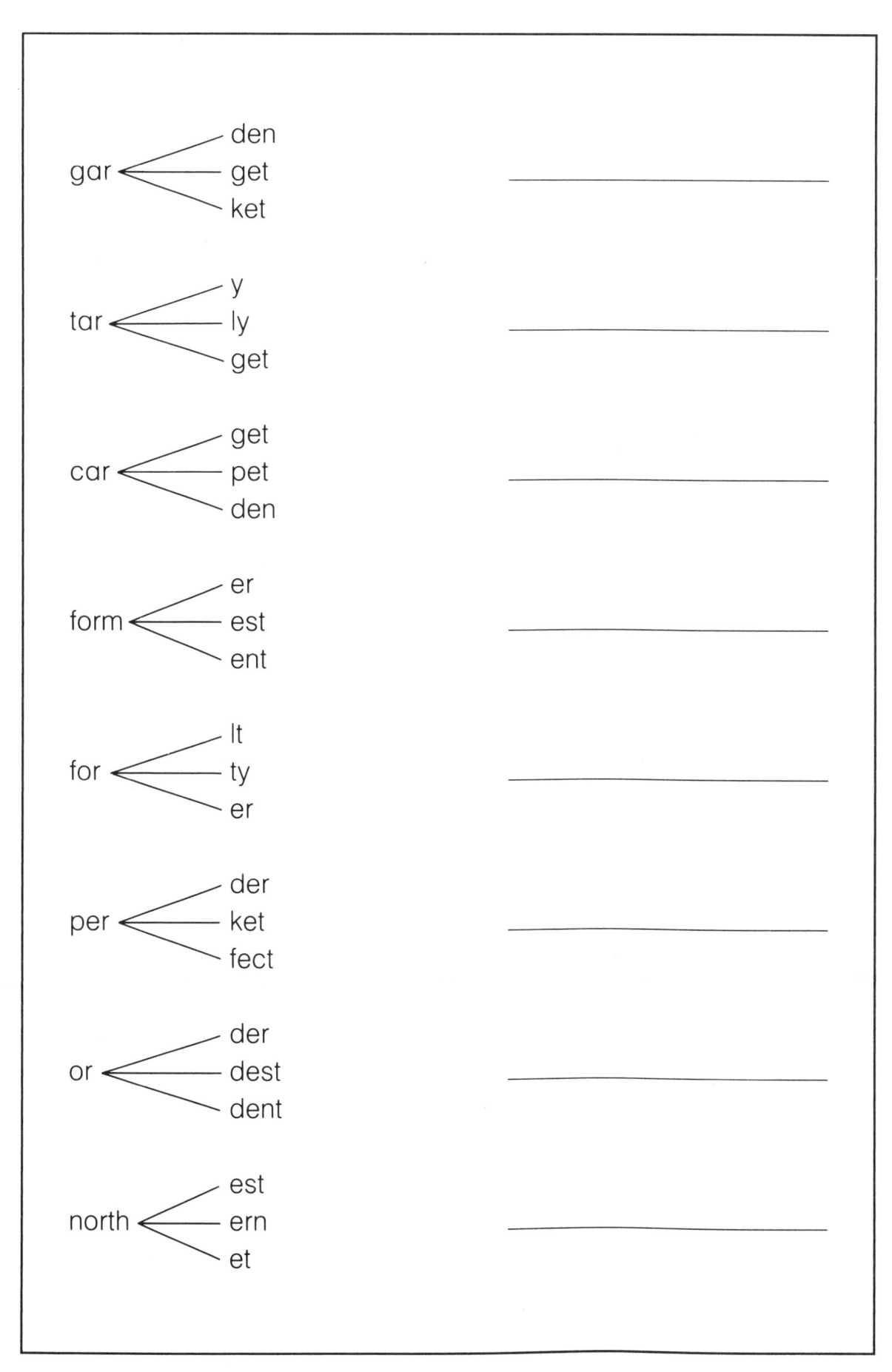

gar → den / get / ket   _____

tar → y / ly / get   _____

car → get / pet / den   _____

form → er / est / ent   _____

for → It / ty / er   _____

per → der / ket / fect   _____

or → der / dest / dent   _____

north → est / ern / et   _____

Note to the teacher
Ask your students to choose an ending to make a new word. They should write this word in the space provided

Word sums mix 'n' match

tar	ling	=	_____
plat	ler	=	_____
a	form	=	_____
hard	den	=	_____
spark	y	=	_____
re	get	=	target
gar	pet	=	_____
car	ly	=	_____
arm	ket	=	_____
mar	larm	=	_____
dar	port	=	_____

Note to the teacher
Ask your students to match the beginnings with the endings to make new words, and then to write the new words after the equals signs. Ask them to make and play a card game, with beginnings and endings on different cards.

50

Writing for meaning

1 Did you hit the tar _____ ?

2 The dog wet the car _____ .

3 We went to shop in the mar _____ .

4 I look at you with _____ larm when you bang the top of your desk.

5 I must go and dig the gar _____ .

6 We can hard _____ go yet.

7 The part _____ must end at ten.

1 In the car you can park your yard.
   You can park your car in the yard.

2 Fangs big sharks have.
   _____

3 Darts go and pubs together.
   _____

4 Go to the must you with the dogs park.
   _____
   _____

5 You cows fields find in.
   _____
   _____

Note to the teacher
Ask your students to complete the words in the first part of the worksheet. In the second part, ask them to unscramble the sentences and then to write them out correctly in the spaces provided.

'want' or 'what' fill'em ups

1 _____ do you _____ for Christmas?

2 _____ do you _____ to do with it?

3 _____ did she say?

4 I don't _____ it.

5 _____ is the good of all this work?

6 _____ a smashing party it was.

7 I do not _____ to wander in the park in the dark.

8 I have _____ you _____ .

9 Do you _____ _____ he has?

10 _____ do you _____ with that?

Note to the teacher
Ask your students to read the sentences and then to choose 'want' or 'what' to complete each one. They should write the chosen word in the blank space and then copy the completed sentence in the space provided.

Wanda the wicked witch

Wanda the wicked witch
lived west of Washington.
She wore a worm as a belt
and on her head a wire wig.
She wanted to wash her wig
so she waved her wand
and her wash tub
filled with warm water.
But as she dropped it
in the tub,
a wild wind blew it away.
Witches must not wash
their wigs on windy, winter
Wednesdays.

Note to the teacher
'Pair read' this passage with your students after they have learned the 'w' rules in *Alpha to Omega*, pp. 52–6.

Wanda's tracking

W	A	N	T	B	P	S	Q	R	W	A	S	P	T	L	G	K	M	E
S	A	V	M	W	H	A	T	J	P	S	N	W	A	S	H	Z	C	I
R	I	N	W	A	R	F	B	I	K	W	A	R	M	D	U	T	O	L
W	A	R	D	V	S	E	H	W	O	R	D	T	U	D	M	P	W	U
G	R	E	W	A	R	D	L	P	I	Y	E	Q	W	O	R	K	V	J
B	T	W	O	R	T	H	V	L	R	W	A	R	N	U	M	O	T	Y
S	I	M	A	R	W	H	A	T	E	V	E	R	K	N	P	O	V	B
W	O	R	L	D	U	H	E	M	L	S	R	T	O	W	A	R	D	S
Y	N	O	T	H	N	K	O	W	A	T	C	H	A	H	P	L	S	N
I	R	W	A	S	E	N	A	Z	I	U	S	I	L	W	A	N	D	R
W	H	A	T	M	O	N	W	A	T	C	H	P	G	U	G	V	C	O
R	I	V	Q	W	O	R	K	B	K	I	K	L	W	O	R	M	R	H
W	O	R	L	D	J	V	Y	P	L	S	B	E	T	O	W	A	R	D
R	O	F	W	A	S	P	T	Q	U	W	A	R	D	H	A	X	T	E
W	A	N	T	B	I	Z	M	W	O	R	D	I	V	W	R	L	P	V
F	O	M	D	W	H	A	T	E	V	E	R	U	S	L	I	M	D	E
P	A	W	A	S	H	R	I	L	T	Y	W	A	R	M	X	T	D	B
B	I	L	A	W	O	R	L	D	J	E	R	L	W	A	S	O	C	R
W	A	N	T	G	T	O	K	D	W	O	R	T	H	Y	F	I	W	H

Note to the teacher
Ask your students to find the 'w' words hidden in this tracking. They should always track from left to right and are not allowed to backtrack. Ask them to circle all the 'w' words and read them aloud when they have finished.

Ask them to track from the top left corner to the bottom right corner. What does it say?

'w' fill'em ups

1 It is too w____m to w_____k in the hot sun.

_____

_____

2 The w____m w_____ks hard to w_____m his way to the top of the grass plot.

_____

_____

3 The First World W_____ started without w_____ning.

_____

_____

4 The witch w____shed her w____g in the hot w____ter.

_____

_____

5 If you w_____k hard with w_____ds, you will find it w_____thwhile.

_____

_____

6 He hid her w____tch to make her mad.

_____

7 You can get a rew_____d for hard w_____k.

_____

_____

8 If I w____nder tow____rd the trash can, I can put this w_____thless w_____k in it.

_____

_____

Note to the teacher
Ask your students to read the sentences and then to complete the 'w' words by filling in 'a', 'ar' or 'or'. Ask them to copy the completed sentences in the spaces provided.

A star is born

TOM

This is the story of Tom. He was ten and he was not very big. He did not think that he was worthy to be a star.

Note to the teacher
This story covers the teaching in *Alpha to Omega* as far as page 57. 'Pair read' it with your students and then ask them to read it on their own. Ask them the questions verbally and then ask them to write the answers down. Finish by discussing the story together. You could start the discussion off by asking such questions as:

Why did Mrs Smith ring 999? Have you ever rung 999?

Have you ever helped on a farm? What did you do?

Chapter 1

It was a fresh wind as Tom went to bring his tent and his camping things in to the shed.

He felt a splash on his chest. It was going to be wet.

"Drat!" he said. "It will drench me." He did not stop till the lot was in. Then he shut the shed with a bang.

He went up to bed and was glum as he held up his damp vest. He did not wish to scrap his next plan. It must not be too wet to go to help his chum.

Chapter 2

Tom jumped up from his bed. He felt that he had not slept a wink. It was six in the morning. Was it wet? He was glad it was not. He had a drink and a sandwich, put his lunch in a bag and then he left in a rush.

He was going to the farm, to help the farmer to cut his corn. It was harvest time. Tom had helped there before. He was not very big, but he was strong and Farmer Smith let him lift and carry. Tom was happy to do such a hard job. But the best job was to bring the men a mug of drink from the charming Mrs. Smith. She had a big slab of plum flan just for Tom.

Chapter 3

It was getting dark and the farm hands had left. Just Farmer Smith and Tom were finishing one corner, before it got darker. There was not much more to do. Then Farmer Smith was going to run Tom to his Mum and Dad.

Suddenly the farmer gave a cry and he slumped over the bag of corn. His arm was trapped in a fan belt. Tom jumped up and went to help him.

Farmer Smith was in a bad way. Tom pushed the 'stop' button and ran to the farm. Mrs. Smith rang 999, then she dashed with Tom to her husband.

Chapter 4

Mrs. Smith's husband was very poorly. Perhaps this was the end. Tom was strong. They must lift Farmer Smith. They must support his limp form, but they must not harm his trapped arm.

Help was at hand before long and the farmer's arm was lifted expertly from the fan belt.

The bell was clanging as they rushed him to hospital. They must not stop for a moment. He was getting worse.

Chapter 5

Farmer Smith did get better. It was thanks to Tom. He had pushed the 'stop' button, and he had run promptly to the farm for help.

Farmer Smith was his friend and he was glad to do his part. He wanted no reward.

When Tom next went to get a mug of drink for the men, Mrs. Smith gave him an extra slab of plum flan for himself and the biggest jug of squash he had ever had. She said he was the best lad in the world.

Questions

1 What was Tom bringing into the shed? Why?

2 What was Tom's next plan?

3 Was it wet when Tom got up in the morning?

4 Where did Tom go?

5 What did Tom do at the farm?

6 What was Tom's best job?

7 What did Mrs. Smith have for Tom?

8 Why did Farmer Smith give a cry?

9 How did Tom help Farmer Smith?

10 Who dashed to help Farmer Smith?

11 What did Tom help to do for Farmer Smith?

12 What was clanging as they rushed to hospital?

13 Did Farmer Smith get better?

14 Did Tom want a reward?

Months of the year

January (1)   February (2)
March (3)   April (4)   May (5)
June (6)   July (7)   August (8)
September (9)   October (10)
November (11)   December (12)

1 Write the names of two months which are often quite cold.

_____   _____

2 Write the names of two months which are often quite hot.

_____   _____

3 Write down the month of your birthday and its number.

_____   _____

4 Three months begin with the same letter. What are they?

_____   _____

_____

5 Which months begin with A?

_____   _____

6 Which months begin with M?

_____   _____

Note to the teacher
'Pair read' this worksheet with your students. Ask them to select and copy the month(s) of the year necessary to complete the blanks.
  Point out that the numbers in brackets refer to the order of the months in the year.

Months and seasons

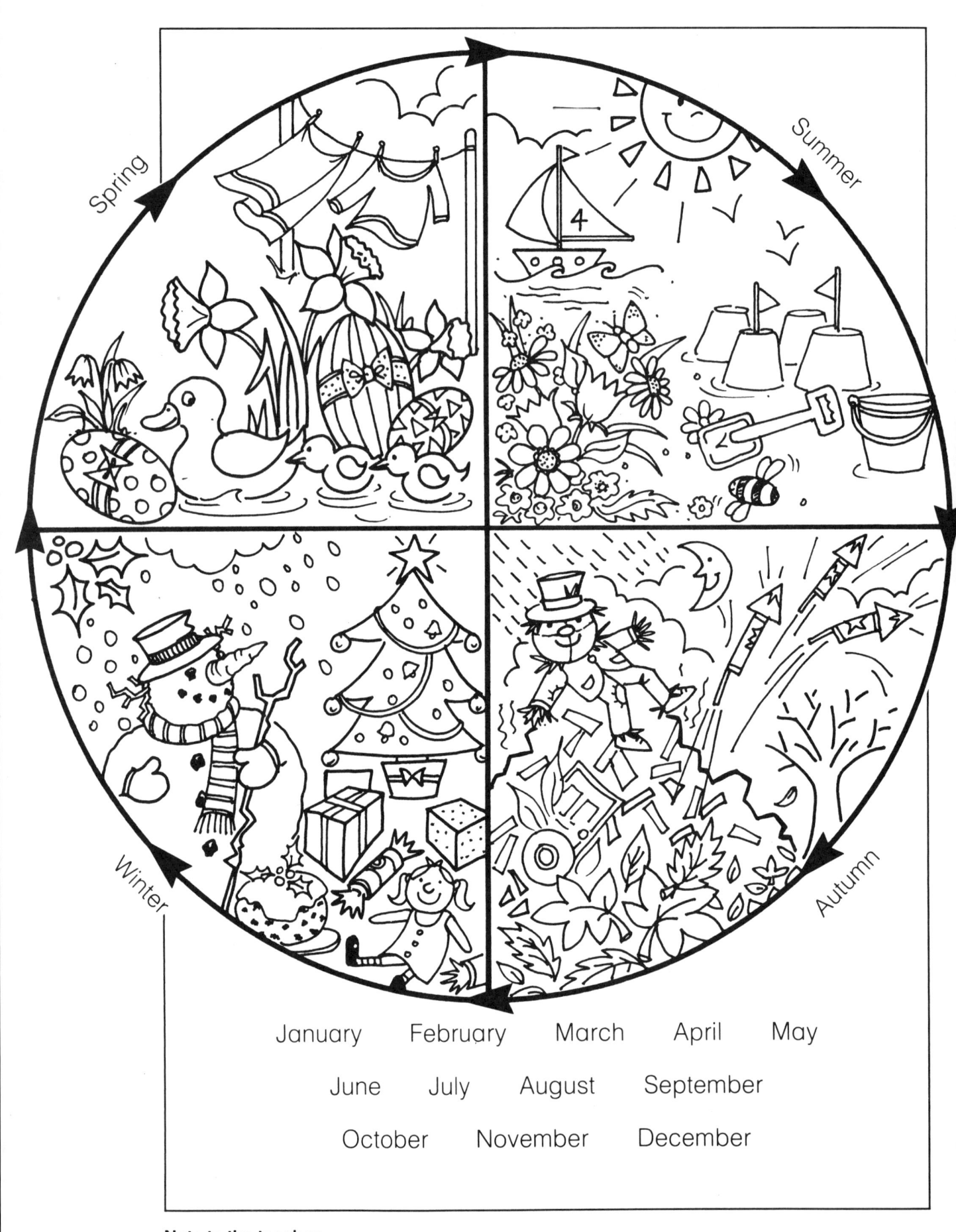

Spring Summer Winter Autumn

January   February   March   April   May

June   July   August   September

October   November   December

Note to the teacher
Provide your students with four coloured pens – brown for autumn, black for winter, green for spring, and blue for summer. Ask them to use the appropriately coloured pen to underline the months that go together and to draw a line from each month to the picture of the season it belongs to.

Months of the year — tracking

A	G	N	J	A	N	U	A	R	Y
D	F	E	B	R	U	A	R	Y	S
O	C	T	I	M	A	R	C	H	O
A	P	R	I	L	D	J	A	N	S
N	O	V	I	B	M	A	Y	S	N
V	I	J	U	N	E	S	E	P	T
M	A	R	W	M	O	J	U	L	Y
K	H	A	U	G	U	S	T	U	R
S	E	P	T	E	M	B	E	R	O
K	P	O	C	T	O	B	E	R	S
A	N	O	V	E	M	B	E	R	T
Q	D	E	C	E	M	B	E	R	G
J	A	N	U	A	R	Y	F	E	B
S	T	F	E	B	R	U	A	R	Y
H	I	M	A	R	C	H	A	P	R
O	U	A	P	R	I	L	A	U	G
M	A	Y	D	E	C	J	U	N	E
J	U	L	Y	O	C	T	Y	O	N
N	O	V	I	A	U	G	U	S	T
F	S	E	P	T	E	M	B	E	R
O	C	T	O	B	E	R	K	I	N
D	A	N	O	V	E	M	B	E	R
L	D	E	C	E	M	B	E	R	J

Note to the teacher
Ask your students to put a circle around each month of the year and each abbreviation (the months are hidden twice). They should track from left to right and are not allowed to backtrack.

Summer holiday

On Sunday we set off for North Sands.
On Monday we went to explore.
On Tuesday the twins swam with armbands.
On Wednesday we dug on the shore.
On Thursday Mum lost her best handbag.
On Friday we had bags of chips.
On Saturday Grandma and Granddad rang up,
And we visited lots of grand ships.

On Sunday we went in to worship.
On Monday we got things to munch.
On Tuesday we went up the river,
And ordered fresh fish for our lunch.
On Wednesday we walked on the sandbank.
On Thursday we went to a farm.
On Friday we picked a big box of red plums.
On Saturday Pat banged her arm.

On Sunday the flag said 'No swimming'.
On Monday we had a bad storm.
On Tuesday we splashed in the water,
But Wednesday began dry and warm.
On Thursday we shopped at the market.
On Friday the twins had a rash.
And Saturday was the sad day to depart,
With five bags, and red spots, and no cash!

Note to the teacher
'Pair read' this story with your students. It includes the sight word 'our'. Ask them the questions verbally and then ask them to write the answers down. Finish by discussing the story together. You could start the discussion off by asking such questions as:

What sort of rash do you think the children might have? Have you ever had a rash? What direction is North Sands, East Sussex, Southampton, West London, etc.?

Questions

1 What did we do on Sunday?

2 Who swam with armbands? When?

3 What did Mum lose on Thursday?

4 When did Grandma and Granddad ring up?

5 What things did we get on Monday?

6 Where did we walk on Wednesday?

7 What did we pick on Friday?

8 What did the flag say on Sunday?

9 When did we splash in the water?

10 Where did we shop on Thursday?

11 What did we depart with on Saturday?

'll' bricks

Rule: When a vowel is short and alone in a one-syllable word, it needs extra help. If the word ends in 'l', write 'll'.

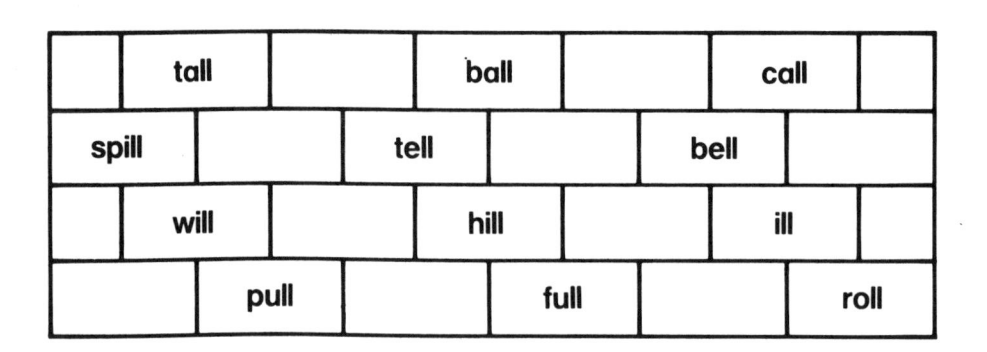

	tall		ball		call	
spill		tell		bell		
	will		hill		ill	
	pull		full		roll	

1 You are a _____ ll boy.

2 The _____ ll on the _____ ll is ringing.

3 She is hot. Can't you _____ ll that she is _____ ll?

4 The bag is _____ ll of shopping. Don't _____ ll on it or it will _____ ll.

5 I _____ ll come home soon.

6 Let's _____ ll the _____ ll down the hill.

7 _____ ll me when you get to the bus stop.

Note to the teacher
Ask your students to read the words in the bricks and the sentences below. Ask them to use one of the words in the bricks to complete the sentences, and then to copy the completed sentences into their exercise books.

'ss' bricks

Rule: When a vowel is short and alone in a one-syllable word, it needs extra help. If the word ends in 's', write 'ss'.

	class		glass		pass	
chess		dress		mess		
	press		loss		boss	
	miss		toss		fuss	

1 Pat has on a red _____ss. It needs a _____.

2 Put the smashed _____ss in the bin. It is a _____ss.

3 You are at the top of the _____ss. You can _____ss the test.

4 He is the _____ss of the shop. He will _____ss if I do not sell the pots of gloss.

5 Don't miss this ball when I _____ss it. It will land in the bush. What a _____ss!

6 Don't _____ss the _____ss match!

Note to the teacher
Ask your students to read the words in the bricks and the sentences below. Ask them to use one of the words in the bricks to complete the sentences, and then to copy the completed sentences into their exercise books.

'ff' bricks

Rule: When a vowel is short and alone in a one-syllable word, it needs extra help. If the word ends in 'f', write 'ff'.

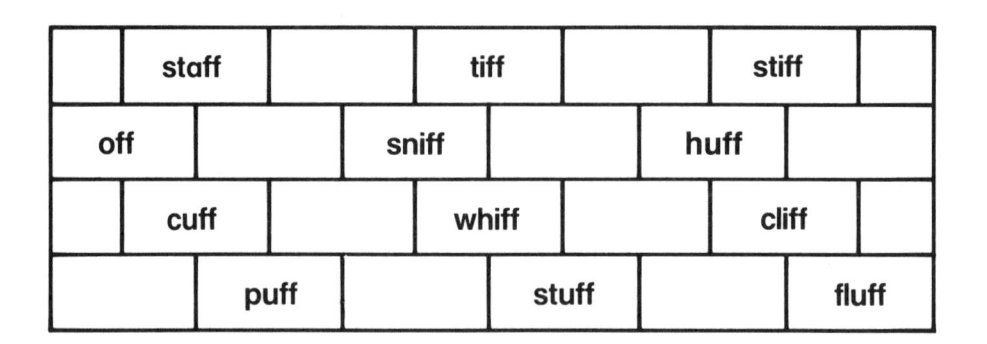

	staff		tiff		stiff	
off		sniff		huff		
	cuff		whiff		cliff	
		puff		stuff		fluff

1 The _____ ff went _____ ff to lunch.

2 The _____ ff on this shirt is _____ ff.

3 Tom and Pam went for a run on the chalk _____ ff. At the top they were huffing and _____ ffing.

4 At the top Tom was cross. They had a _____ ff. Pam went off in a _____ ff.

5 I will help Mum to _____ ff a bit of lamb for Sunday lunch.

6 Jan's hat has large balls of _____ ff on it. They are red and tan.

7 Did you get a _____ ff of the lamb I _____ ffed being cooked for lunch?

Note to the teacher
Ask your students to read the words in the bricks and the sentences below. Ask them to use one of the words in the bricks to complete the sentences, and then to copy the completed sentences into their exercise books.

Flossy words

ff   ll   ss

Balloons: tell spell yell | tiff off huff | grill will fill | press dress mess | sniff puff stuff | grass moss gloss

He is very tall!

1 The witch will **tell** you her _____ if you do not _____ .

2 The fish on the **grill** _____ _____ us up.

3 **Press** the _____ . It is in a _____ .

4 When it is wet, the **grass** and the _____ have a _____ .

5 Don't **sniff** or _____ this _____ .

6 They had a **tiff** and he went _____ in a _____ .

Note to the teacher
The students should match the words in each balloon with the sentence to which it belongs. The students should write the words into the sentence – the first word in each case has been done for them.
  More words and dictation are in *Alpha to Omega*, pp. 58–70.

Tim in the fog

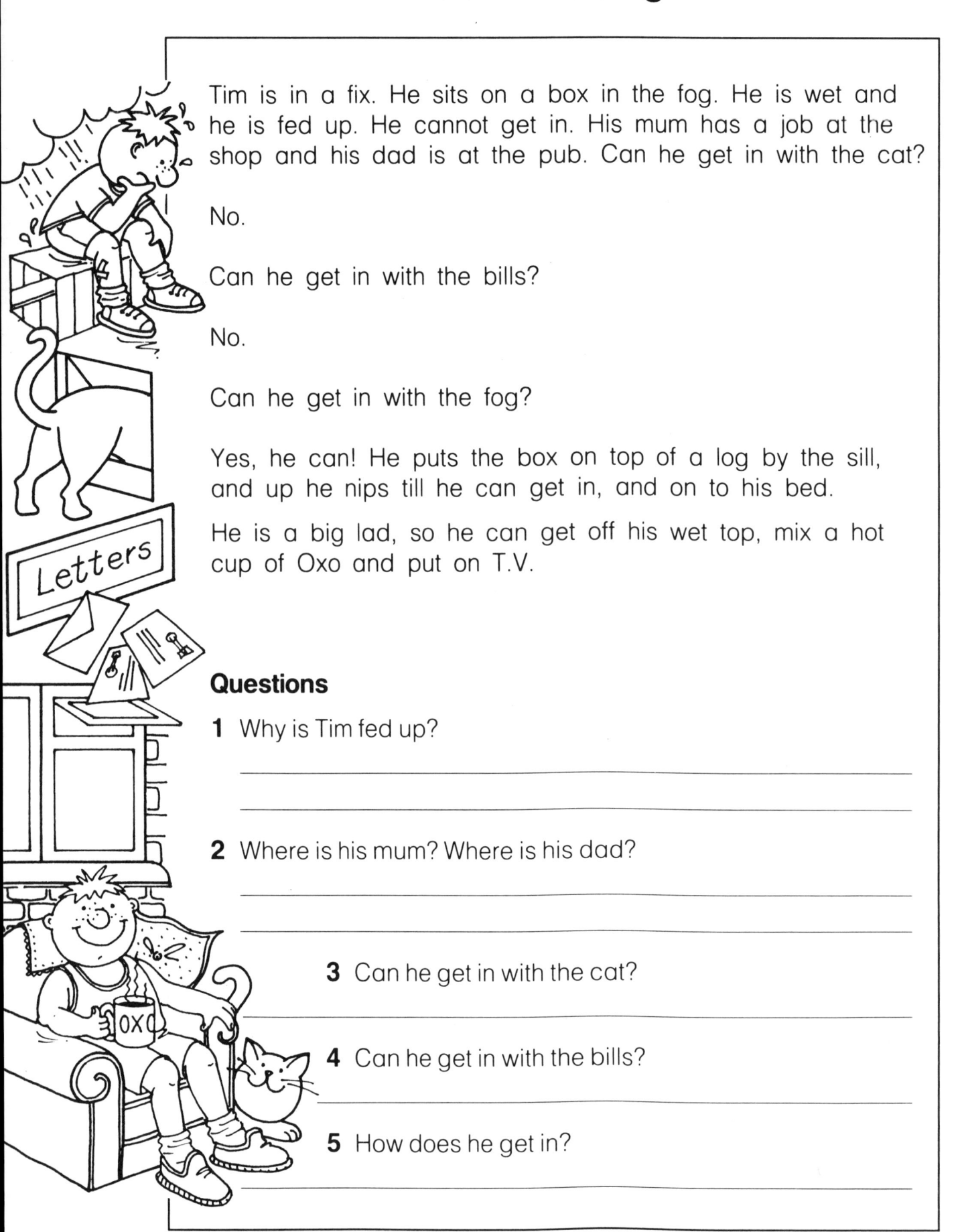

Tim is in a fix. He sits on a box in the fog. He is wet and he is fed up. He cannot get in. His mum has a job at the shop and his dad is at the pub. Can he get in with the cat?

No.

Can he get in with the bills?

No.

Can he get in with the fog?

Yes, he can! He puts the box on top of a log by the sill, and up he nips till he can get in, and on to his bed.

He is a big lad, so he can get off his wet top, mix a hot cup of Oxo and put on T.V.

Questions

1 Why is Tim fed up?

2 Where is his mum? Where is his dad?

3 Can he get in with the cat?

4 Can he get in with the bills?

5 How does he get in?

Note to the teacher
'Pair read' this 'll' story with your students. Ask the questions verbally and then ask them to write down the answers. Finish by discussing the story with them.

'they' or 'there' fill'em ups

1 _____ went _____ with Bill.

2 Did _____ say that the man went _____?

3 _____ _____ are after all!

4 _____ all went _____ in Bill's car.

5 Can _____ park _____?

6 The men are _____.

7 _____ are not _____ yet.

8 Where are _____?

9 _____ are over _____.

10 _____ went over _____ with them.

11 _____ went on the bus to get _____.

12 Who are _____ standing with over _____?

13 Let's go over _____ with them.

14 _____ _____ are sitting on the bench in the park.

15 _____ we are; it's all over.

Note to the teacher
Ask your students to read the sentences and then to choose 'they' or 'there' to complete each one. They should write the chosen word in the blank space and then copy the completed sentences into their exercise books.

Short forms roundabouts

I am not well.
I'm not well.

1 He is top of the list.

2 She is too fat.

3 He is a bad lot.

4 We are all going with you.

5 They are all in the hall.

6 You will not be going to the party.

7 You are the best person in the form.

8 Do not do that.

9 I cannot do it.

10 I will not do it.

Note to the teacher
Ask your students to replace the verb in each sentence with its short form and then to rewrite the sentence below its original in the space provided.

Short forms roundabouts

**I'm very hot.
I am very hot.**

1 I'm so fed up.
_____

2 He's drunk, I think.
_____

3 We're not very well.
_____

4 You're a pig.
_____

5 They'll never win.
_____

**The trunk belongs to Bill.
It belongs to him.
It is his.**

1 The hat belongs to Jim.
_____
_____

2 The bag belongs to Mum.
_____
_____

Note to the teacher
Ask your students to replace the verb in sentences 1–5 with its expanded form and then to rewrite the sentence below its original in the space provided.
  Ask them to scale down the last two sentences, using possessive pronouns.

Short forms roundabouts

He can come for a walk.
He can't come for a walk.

1 Jim is the best runner in my form.

2 This is the longest scarf in the world.

3 Pam was the worst at sport.

4 I can go to the ball.

5 Sam and Pam will be going at six.

Note to the teacher
Ask your students to replace the verb in each sentence with its negative short form and to rewrite the sentences below their original in the spaces provided.

Short forms roundabouts

**I have not spent all my cash.
I have spent all my cash.**

1 Dad will not lend the car to Ben.

_____

2 Mum has not lost her hat.

_____

3 Len won't run over the dog.

_____

4 I can't be at Bob's by ten.

_____

5 I won't be going to the party.

_____

6 I don't think that remark upset her.

_____

Note to the teacher
Ask your students to replace the negative verb in each sentence with its affirmative form and then to rewrite the sentence below its original in the space provided.

'ss' fill'em ups

class brass glass grass
lass   pass   dress less
miss   floss toss   fuss

1 I want a _____ of water.

2 I have more than Pam, so she has _____ than me.

3 _____ me the salt.

4 The door knob is _____ .

5 Bess is a big _____ .

6 I want some candy _____ .

7 We go to _____ in the morning.

8 When he left her, she made a _____ .

9 Did you _____ the bus today?

10 I saw him _____ the ball at the car.

11 Do not walk on the _____ .

12 She has on a red _____ for the party.

Note to the teacher
Ask your students to read the sentences and then to choose an 'ss' word to complete each one. They should write the chosen word in the blank space and then copy the completed sentences into their exercise books.

'of', 'off' or 'for' fill'em ups

1 She fell _____ the top _____ the flats.

2 We must be _____ , it's half past ten.

3 We went on top _____ the bus _____ a bit.

4 You must take _____ your dress before you jump into bed _____ the night.

5 Get _____ your bike and get me a bag _____ crisps from that shop. I want them _____ tea.

6 I have a lot _____ sums to do.

7 The alarm went _____ at six. _____ once it woke me up.

8 You are at the top _____ the class. Go _____ it!

9 I went to work _____ a farmer. He kept five _____ his pigs _____ food.

10 Ben got _____ the bus _____ a bit _____ a walk.

11 I smell lots _____ bits _____ us to eat before we are _____ to bed.

12 The cat sat in front _____ the car _____ an hour. Then he ran _____ .

Note to the teacher
Ask your students to read the sentences and then to choose 'of', 'off' or 'for' to complete each one. They should write the chosen word in the blank space and then copy the completed sentences into their exercise books.

'c', 'k' or 'ck' fill'em ups

1 This must be the wrong tra ____ , it is just a mud path.

2 Can you go to the ban ____ for me and get the cash?

3 I do want a drin ____ of water.

4 Ja ____ put the sa ____ on his ba ____ and went off with the stuff.

5 I want a boo ____ to loo ____ at.

6 The lad pi ____ ed up a thi ____ sti ____ and hit the ball with a ____ rack.

7 ____ luck, ____ luck went the hen as we fed her.

8 I have a han ____ y in my po ____ et.

9 We ran qui ____ ly when the ro ____ et went off.

10 The cri ____ et match was called off as the wi ____ et was wet.

11 The lo ____ et was on her ne ____ when it fell off.

12 What a bit of lu ____ ! We ki ____ ed it up on the river ban ____ .

13 The bu ____ et is under the sin ____ .

14 I thin ____ you will need a thi ____ ja ____ et when it is windy.

Note to the teacher
Ask your students to read the sentences and then to choose 'c', 'k' or 'ck' to complete each one. They should write the chosen letter(s) in the blank space and then copy the completed sentences into their exercise books.

'ck' or 'nk' fill'em ups

Rule: Words ending **'ck'** are also 'flossy' words because you need two **'k'** sounds if the vowel is short and alone.

Short and alone	Not alone
back	bank
black	blank
rack	rank
brick	brink
lick	link
sick	sink
thick	think
clock	clonk

1 I thi _____ that stick is thi _____ .

2 The clo _____ fell off the wall and went clo _____ .

3 He put his cash ba _____ in the ba _____ .

4 The bla _____ film was bla _____ .

5 His jacket is on the first ra _____ of ra _____ s.

6 The bri _____ was on the bri _____ of falling off the wall.

7 Li _____ the bits to li _____ them together.

8 Nick was si _____ in the si _____ .

Note to the teacher
Ask your students to read the lists out loud and then to choose 'ck' or 'nk' to complete the sentences below. (The words listed will give them a clue.) They should write the chosen letters in the blank space and then copy the completed sentences into their exercise books.

'ed', 'ing' or 'et' fill'em ups

1 The ship will be dock _____ at ten o'clock.

2 I was shock _____ by that nasty remark.

3 Bill pick _____ the man's pock _____ and got a wad of cash.

4 This is a lock _____ for your neck.

5 Do not kick the buck _____ just yet!

6 Just my luck to be track _____ the wrong chap!

7 The ducks are quack _____ on the pond; they want to be fed.

8 That is a nasty mark on your jack _____ , Jock.

9 That pin is prick _____ me.

10 Jack and Pat are neck _____ in the back of the car.

11 We all flock _____ to the shock _____ film.

12 You will get fat after tuck _____ in to so much grub.

13 The poor chicken is pluck _____ for lunch.

14 What we are lack _____ is one thick stock _____ .

15 The boss sack _____ Bill for not going to work.

16 This cup is crack _____ .

Note to the teacher
Each sentence contains a word spelled with 'ck' which needs the ending 'ed', 'ing' or 'et'. Ask your students to read the sentences and then to choose one of these endings so the sentences make sense. They should write the chosen ending in the blank space and then copy the completed sentences into their exercise books.

'f' and 'th'
'v' and 'TH'

Lots of us have difficulty saying 'f' and 'th' and 'v' and 'TH' in the right places. Now is the time to get it right! Look in a mirror and put your top teeth on your bottom lip. Say 'f'. Now put your tongue between your top and bottom teeth and look in the mirror again. Say 'th'. Now look in the mirror and practise saying 'f', 'th', 'f', 'th', lots of times.

Now do the same exercises with 'v' and 'TH'. This time you will hear the sounds, not just feel them.

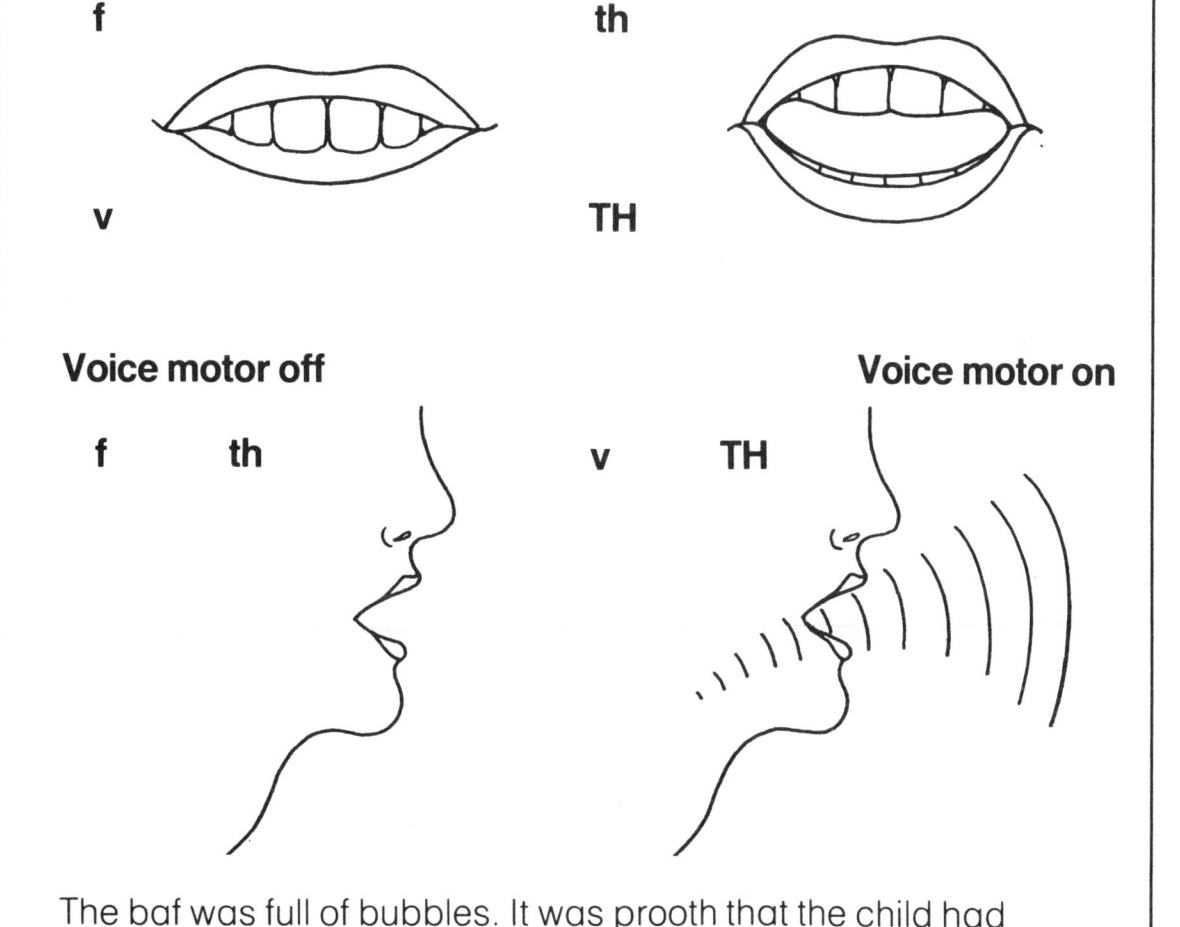

f th

v TH

Voice motor off **Voice motor on**

f th v TH

The baf was full of bubbles. It was prooth that the child had put too much thoam in the water. His mover was thurious wiv him.

Note to the teacher
When your students have thoroughly practised the different sounds, ask them to correct the mistakes in the paragraph at the bottom of the sheet.

'th'
not 'f' or 'v'

Smi _____

some _____ ing

wi _____

Saman _____ a

no _____ ing

fur _____ er

fa _____ er

_____ eatre

_____ rush

wea _____ er

mo _____ er

fea _____ ered

_____ umb

bro _____ er

any _____ ing

whe _____ er

ba _____

_____ ought

Samanfa and her mover, faver and brover went to the featre. Nofing went right. The weaver was bad. Samanfa wanted somefing to drink, but she couldn't find anyfing. Her brover Tom fell in a hole and went furver and furver down. Mr. and Mrs. Smif, Samanfa's parents, could do nofing for him. They didn't know whever they should hold onto one fumb or the over. Somefing had to happen soon or he would have had a baf wif his fine-feavered friends. Soon a frush came along and plucked him out. Samanfa and Tom never fought of going to the featre again.

Note to the teacher
Ask your students to fill in the 'th' missing from each word and then to read the word aloud. Ask them to proofread the final paragraph and to correct all the mis-spelled words. They should then copy the corrected version into their exercise books.

Words you need to know

I **say** to you,
"Be good."

He **says** to me,
"Be better."

She **said** to everyone,
"Be best."

"Where are you going to,
my pretty maid?"
"I'm going a-milking,
Sir," she said.

Note to the teacher
'Pair read' this sheet with your students and then ask them to read it out loud by themselves. (In the rhyme, pronounce 'said' like 'maid' to help them remember the spelling.)

Make sure your students learn to spell each word thoroughly using the 'read, spell, cover, spell again with eyes closed, write and check' technique.

Words you need to know

He **should** get out. He **would** get out, if he **could** get out – oh you, lonely duck.

o u l d

o u l d

o u lonely duck

We would like a bit of ham.
We could take it from the can,
we should put it in the pan.
When it's hot,
we could eat a lot.
We would have a bit,
but it should not make us sick.

Tom would be sad if he hit Dad.
Dad should be mad.
He could grab the lad.

Note to the teacher
'Pair read' this sheet with your students and then ask them to read it out loud by themselves, and to colour in the big letters.
  Make sure your students learn to spell each word thoroughly using the 'read, spell, cover, spell again with eyes closed, write and check' technique. Use the sentences for dictation.

The Highway Code

Do you know these road signs?

No right turn    **STOP**    **Roundabout**

Circles give orders.
Red circles mean you **must not**.   Blue circles mean you **must**.

Motor vehicles prohibited    **No U turn**    **No cycling**

No left turn    **Ahead only**    **Turn left ahead**

Triangles give a warning.

Level crossing    **T junction**    **Wild animals**

Slippery road    **Road works**    **Falling rocks**

Squares give information.

Parking    **Hospital ahead**    **Route recommended for cyclists**

No through road    **Temporary lane closure**    **One-way traffic**

Note to the teacher
This is primarily an information sheet for older students who are learning the Highway Code. Ask them to colour the signs in the appropriate colours. They could play a B and C road sign pairs game.

Talk skills

A picture to tell about.

Note to the teacher
Ask your students to describe what is happening in the picture.
Use it to start a discussion. Ask them to describe in writing what is taking place.

'e' can be magic too

It makes the other vowel say its name.

I hate that hat.

He rips the skin from the ripe plum.

She said it was not a love note.

A tube of explosive was hidden in the tub.

Note to the teacher
Dictate the sentences to your students. Ask them to mark the long vowels with a macron (¯) and the short vowels with a breve (˘).

Do all the dictations in *Alpha to Omega* pp. 77–79, and ask your students to write a story bringing in as many "magic 'e'" words as they can.

Magic 'e' fill'em ups

1 fame   tame   shame
He wants _____ .

2 lake   wake   game
She came for a _____ all the same.

3 quake   date   fate
You are late for the _____ that we made.

4 mate   late   gate
Shut the _____ .

5 snake   safe   shake
Put this in the _____ .

6 maze   craze   laze
Have you sent Dad to the _____ ? He will get lost.

7 care   fare   mare
The bus _____ has just gone up.

8 stale   ale   sale
Mum and Dad went to the pub for some _____ .

9 hate   bathe   ate
We can _____ in this lake.

10 rake   make   fake
Can you _____ me a lemon cake?

11 tape   nape   cape
Put on the _____ so we can sing.

Note to the teacher
Ask your students to choose one of the words above each sentence and to write it in the blank space to complete the sentence. They should copy the completed sentences into their exercise books.

Statements into questions

You think he is a brave man.
Do you think he is a brave man?

1 This class had to work.

_____

2 She had to park there.

_____

3 We went for a ride in the car.

_____

4 Sam picks up his chicken in his fingers.

_____

_____

5 I care when you make mistakes.

_____

Note to the teacher
Ask your students to make the statements into questions using the auxiliary ('helper') verb 'to do'.

Questions into statements

Did you have a bad day?
You had a bad day.

1 Did you make these stale cakes?

2 Do you care what you put on in the morning?

3 Does your father shave every day?

4 Does Dick tell bad jokes?

5 Did you put these things over here?

6 Does she tell you where she is going?

Note to the teacher
Ask your students to turn the questions back into statements.

Statements into questions

He chose that rose.
He chose that rose, didn't he?

You mustn't pose like that.
You mustn't pose like that, must you?

1 We got lost in the maze.

2 Tom has a big nose.

3 My cake won't rise.

4 He is a wise man.

5 It's just a bit of wasteland.

6 We didn't bathe in the lake.

7 It was fun on the slide.

8 She is a good woman.

Note to the teacher
Ask your students to turn the statements into questions by adding a 'tag'.

9 I'm not sickening for 'flu.

10 You haven't woken her up.

11 Golf is a craze with him.

12 A wave of crime has hit England.

13 Wales isn't my homeland.

14 You will choke if you drink so fast.

15 He didn't get the prize.

16 You can't help me with this lot.

Statements into questions

who   what   whose   which   when

Jane made the beds.
Who **made the beds?**

1 The dog bit him.

2 Charles wants a turn on the slide.

3 My book got torn.

4 The slide belongs to me. (whose)

5 The bus takes us to school in the morning.

6 The black cat is resting on the brick wall. (which)

7 Jan went to visit her grandmother on Sunday.

8 Kim's red car is in the race. (whose)

9 The black party dress is on Pat's bed. (which)

Note to the teacher
Ask your students to turn the statements into questions by using 'question words' beginning with 'wh'.

Soft 'c' and 'g'

Now we will tell you when **c** says 's' and **g** says 'j':

e i y

are the vowels that work this magic.

The city gent sat in the centre of the circle and wished he had a sack of gems for his gentle Grace.

Now you can work out why some words begin with 'k' or 'j'.

Judy jumped when kind King Ken dumped his jam tarts at her feet.
"Just for you," he said, "my sweet. Kippers are my joy for a treat."

Note to the teacher
This sheet is an introduction to the softening effect of certain vowels on specific consonants, examined more fully in *Alpha to Omega*, pp. 92–106.

Ask your students to read the nonsense verses and to colour in the large letters. They could play the *Alpha to Omega* Flashcard games (see pp. 94 and 102).

'k', 'c' or 'ck' fill'em ups

1 __ ut a sli __ e of __ a __ e for Grace.

2 She can dan __ e with gra __ e and charm.

3 His name is __ en.

4 The __ ing was __ ind to his subjects.

5 He is not that __ ind of man.

6 If I s __ ip lunch, I will have time to go to the shops.

7 Bla __ is the opposite of white.

8 The __ at fell into the cra __ in the __ ellar wall.

9 The ra __ e for first pla __ e was won by the Es __ imo.

10 I took a chan __ e on roman __ e at the dan __ e.

11 The staff at the pala __ e were __ een to give the __ ing the servi __ e he wanted.

12 The servi __ e at the mar __ et is ex __ ellent.

13 His re __ ent ac __ ident s __ arred his s __ in.

14 It would be ni __ e to s __ ip this dan __ e.

Note to the teacher
Ask your students to read the sentences and then to choose 'k', 'c' or 'ck' to complete each one. They should write the chosen letter(s) in the blank space and then copy the completed sentences into their exercise books.

'to be' + 'ing'

The podgy lodger ate all my fudge.
The podgy lodger is eating **all my fudge.**

1 I made this stodgy cake.

2 We went to Cambridge for a short while.

3 I will wedge the door with this.

4 The blazing plane went over the ridge.

5 I made a budget and stuck to it.

6 Dad planted the hedge to stop the badgers.

7 We pulled our sledge to the top of the ridge for a fast run.

Note to the teacher
Ask your students to change these sentences into the present continuous tense by using the 'helper verb' 'to be' and by adding 'ing' to the main verb. They should copy the completed sentences into their exercise books.

Checklist for *Alpha to Omega*: Stage One

Page	Concept	Sheet No.	Already known	Taught	Revised	Secure
22	Short vowels	7, 13				
21	Consonants	4				
30–1	Consonant digraphs	19–25				
23	'y' as a consonant/vowel	7				
23–4	Short vowel words	8a–b, 9				
23–4	Closed syllables	6a–b, 8a–b, 9				
23–5	Open syllables: 'be', etc. Sentences Full stops Capitals	11, 12				
26–7	Questions Plurals – suffix 's'	10				
28–31	2 consonant blends 3 consonant blends	19–25 31–35				
36–7	'mp', 'nd', 'nt', 'nch'	39, 42				
38	Closed syllable word sums	43				
40–2	'ng', 'ngk'	42b				
42–3	Past tense 'ed' (id, t, d)	89				
43–5	'ar'	45a, 46–50				
45–6	Vowel + 'r' syllables Word sums	45a–b, 46, 47, 50 48, 49				
48–50	'or' and 'er' 'er' as a suffix 'or', 'er' word sums	45b, 47 45b, 47 48, 49				
52–3	'w' rule 1 – 'wa' Short forms – wasn't, it's	52–54				
53–4	'qua' Transformations	83–85				
54–5	want, what 'w' rule 2 – 'war'	51 53, 54				
56	'w' rule 3 – 'wor'	53, 54				
57	Abbreviations Can't, won't	66, 68, 69				
58–60	'll' 'll' word sums	60, 63, 64				

Note to the teacher
This checklist is to help the teacher keep a record of the concepts each student has learned while progressing through *Alpha to Omega*. It is based on the Fourth Edition.

Page	Concept	Sheet No.	Already known	Taught	Revised	Secure
60	they, there Short forms – is, will	65 66–69				
61	Possessive pronoun	67				
62	'al' saying /aw/					
63	Homonyms Transformations: negative and short forms	66–69				
64–6	'ss', 'zz' Exceptions: bus, etc.	61, 70				
67–8	'as' saying /ars/					
69–70	'ff'	62, 63				
69	Exceptions: if, of, etc. 'a' after 'f' saying /ar/ 'a' before 'th' saying /ar/					
71–5	'ck' Suffixes 'ed', 'ing', 'et'	72, 73 74				
76	Reminder of long vowel sounds	81, 82				
77–9	Silent 'e' a–e	81, 82				
79–81	e–e					
80–1	Statements into questions	83				
81–3	i–e					
83–4	o–e					
85	u–e					
88–9	Story writing More statements into questions	85a–b				
89–91	'v' rule Short forms: I've, etc. 'wh' revision	86				
91	'o' saying /u/ – love					
92	Transformations: negative Negative question					
92	Concept of antonyms, synonyms					
92–3	The 'k' sound Soft 'c' before 'e', 'i', ('y')	88 87				

90c

Page	Concept	Sheet No.	Already known	Taught	Revised	Secure
92–3	Initial soft 'c'	87, 88				
94–5	Medial soft 'c'	88				
95–6	Final soft 'c'	88				
97–9	When to use 'k' The 'g' sound	88				
99	Initial soft 'g' Exceptions: got, etc.	87				
100	Medial soft 'g'					
101–2	Final soft 'g'					
105	'j'					
106–8	'Walls'					
106	'gu'					
107	Present continuous 'ing'	89				
107–8	'dge'	89				
108	'tch'					
108	Exceptions: much, etc.					
109	Ind, int, ild old, ost					
111	Spelling Test, Stage 1					

Checklist copyright © Patience Thomson 1981